Van Gogh

Van Gogh

R.J.M. Philpott

Series Editors
Michael and Mollie Hardwick

Evergreen Lives

ISBN 0 7127 0002 1

Series Editors
Michael and Mollie Hardwick

Design by Roy Lee

Production by Bob Towell

Colour Separations
by
D.S. Colour International Limited, London
Photo-typesetting
by
Sayers Clark Limited, Croydon, Surrey

Printed and bound in Spain by
TONSA, San Sebastian

Contents

Select Bibliography

J.-B. DE LA FAILLE - *The Works of Vincent van Gogh* (London 1970).

J. PATRICE MARENDEL - *Great Masterpieces by van Gogh* (New York 1979).

LARA VINCA MASINI - Van Gogh (London 1967).

CARL NORDENFALK - *The Life and Work of van Gogh* (London 1953).

G. POLLOCK & F. ORTON - *Vincent van Gogh: Artist of his Time* (London 1978).

MARK ROSKILL - *Van Gogh, Gauguin and the Impressionist Circle* (London 1970).

MARC EDO TRALBAUT - *Vincent van Gogh* (London 1969).

VINCENT VAN GOGH - *Complete Letters* (London and New York 1958).

ROBERT WALLACE - *The World of van Gogh: 1853-1890* (New York & London 1969).

Chronology

1853 Vincent Willem van Gogh born at Groot Zundert, Brabant, Holland, 30 March.

1857 Vincent's brother Theo born 1 May.

1869 Vincent joins Goupil's art gallery in The Hague in July.

1872 His lifelong correspondence with Theo begins.

1873 Transferred to Goupil's London branch. Rejected in love by his landlady's daughter, Eugénie Loyer.

1874 Moves to the Goupil head office in Paris in October, returning to London in December. Becomes preoccupied with religion.

1875 Returns to Paris in May, his interest in art intensifying.

1876 Dismissed by Goupil, returns to England for a teaching appointment at Ramsgate, Kent, then becomes assistant to a Methodist minister, Mr Jones, at Isleworth, West London.

1877 Works briefly in a bookshop at Dordrecht,

Holland. Moves to Amsterdam in May to study theology for University entrance examination.

1878 Abandons his studies in July to attend a mission school near Brussels. Fails to qualify and in December becomes an evangelist in the Borinage mining district near Mons.

1880 After long deprivation moves to Brussels to begin art studies. Theo begins sending him an allowance.

1881 Returns to his parents' home near Etten, in south Holland. Rejected in love by his widowed cousin Kee Vos. Settles in The Hague, taking painting lessons from Anton Mauve, after breaking with his father and abandoning religious interests.

1882 Shares his lodging with a prostitute, Sien Hoornik, becoming absorbed in painting.

1883 Parts from Sien in September and moves to Drenthe, north Holland, with ideals of an artists' colony. Attempts reconciliation with his parents at Nuenen, near Etten, at Christmas.

1884 A middle-aged neighbour, Margot Bege-mann, attempts suicide when he rejects her love.

1885 His father dies suddenly, 26 March. Vincent moves to Antwerp in November.

1886 Joins Antwerp Academy of Art but soon leaves, to share Theo's Paris lodgings. Attends Cormon's studio and makes friends with Emile Bernard, Lautrec, Signard and other progressives. His technique developing rapidly.

1888 Moves to Arles in South of France in

February. Takes the 'Yellow House', where Gauguin joins him. Their quarrels lead to Vincent's first breakdown, when he mutilates his ear; but it is the most prolific period of his art.

1889 Local hostility results in further traumas and periods in hospital. He voluntarily enters the asylum at Saint-Remy in May. Theo marries Johanna van Bonger.

1890 Theo's child born 1 February. Vincent's work seems about to gain recognition. His last visits to Paris. Places himself under medical supervision of Dr Gachet at Auvers, Provence, painting some of his greatest works. Becoming more depressed, he shoots himself, dying 29 July.

1891 Theo dies.

Introduction

HIS PAINTINGS HANG among the treasures of the world's most famed galleries; but it is possible to pass a lifetime without ever visiting an art gallery yet still appreciate the works of Vincent van Gogh. In count-less homes and public places reproductions of them are so familiar as to seem part of the furniture. The yellow blaze of *Sunflowers* ('How beautiful yellow is!' he said), his own *Chair and Pipe*, the portrait of Armand Roulin, the postman's son, in his black hat and yellow jacket, rugged old Patience Escalier: they are bearers of light and cheerfulness into places that might be very drab without them. 'I want to make drawings that *touch* some people,' he wrote. 'I want to reach so far that people will say of my work: he feels deeply, he feels tenderly.'

Yet the man who bountifully scattered his gifts on the world, gifts of glorious colour and form, delight-ing and enriching the eye and spirit, endured for most of his thirty-seven years an existence of strug-gle and mental suffering almost without parallel. Far more typical of him than the 'pretty' works is that self-portrait in which he looks out on the beholder, sideways, suspicious, like a trapped animal, pipe desperately puffing out smoke, as though it were a consolation during torture; and beneath the fur cap, round the side of his face, a bandage concealing the ear he had himself mutilated - why?

That Vincent van Gogh was born a Dutchman was one of nature's ironies. The European country noted for the phlegmatic temperament of its people produced, in 1853, one who wore his spirit on the outside; a naked soul vulnerable from childhood to the impact of harsh experience and tormented by ideals and aspirations he felt but could hardly understand or express. 'What am I in the eyes of most people? a nobody, or an eccentric and dis-agreeable man... the lowest of the low,' he said at one time; and at another, 'How, then, might I be of use? What purpose might I serve? There is some-thing within me, but what is it? Men are often powerless to do anything, prisoners of some horrible, horrible cage!'

What was within him was Art, the genius which would inspire him to paint with such power and pass-ion that it would seem his eyes, like Turner's before him, were made in a different way from those of other people. But before he could make this discovery he was to suffer, lost and bewildered in a world he did not understand and which did not understand him. His lot was made harder by the strain of madness which ran in his family, showing itself in a sister and brother after it had destroyed him.

At first, finding no fulfilment in the picture-deal-ing to which his family had hopefully apprenticed him, he turned to human love. 'It is good to love as much as one can, for it is here that true strength lies; he who loves much is capable of great things and accomplishes them, and what is done through love is done well.' But the girl, his London landlady's daughter, of whose love he was utterly confident (for surely she must feel the strength of his own), failed to reciprocate. He was dashed, humiliated.

Inner compulsions turned him to a broader kind of love. Vincent was essentially, leaving out the flaw of inherited madness and the great gift of Art, a saint. He despised or ignored worldly things, comforts, his own appearance. Now he saw it as his vocation to go among the poorest and most deprived people he could meet, to comfort and to preach to them. At first he worked in England, not very successfully, then among the wretched coalminers of the Borin-age district, near Mons, teaching the children, visit-ing the sick, reading the Bible to them and to himself,

and writing, always writing letters to his brother
Theo, the closest person to him in the world; letters
so innocently profound, so deeply sincere and self-
revealing, that they stand completely independent
of his paintings as records of his soul. Theo, his
junior in years, played an almost parental part to
the young man whose own parents found him incomprehensible. It was Theo (whose own letters to
Vincent have most regrettably been lost) who
listened patiently, advised, encouraged, and constantly sent money to one who would never earn a
living for himself.

But in the Borinage Vincent failed to fit in. The
authorities were not satisfied, and dismissed him.
From this time comes one of his most deep and self-
analytical letters to Theo:

> ...you must not think that I disavow things; I am
> rather faithful in my unfaithfulness, and though
> changed, I am the same, and my only anxiety is:
> how can I be of use in the world, cannot I serve
> some purpose and be of any good, how can I learn
> more and study certain subjects profoundly? You
> see, that is what preoccupies me constantly, and
> then I feel myself imprisoned by poverty, exclud-
> ed from participating in certain work... That is
> one reason for not being without melancholy, and
> then one feels an emptiness where there might be
> friendship and strong and serious affections, and
> one feels a terrible discouragement gnawing at one's
> very moral energy, and fate seems to put a barrier
> to the instincts of affection, and a flood of disgust
> rises to choke one. And one exclaims "How long,
> my God?"

Not long, it proved. Soon he was telling Theo, 'I will
take up my pencil, which I have forsaken in my dis-
couragement, and I will go on with my drawing.' He
had been drawing all the time, studies of miners in
their bleak ugly landscape, going to the shaft, digging and heaving coal; dark sketches in various media,
including black lithographic crayon, pen and brush.
They contained no hint of what was to come.

In his wanderings he found two more women, his

widowed cousin Kee, who rejected him, and 'Sien', an unhappy prostitute whom he contemplated marrying, and whose bastard child he loved as his own. She refused to join him when he decided to move to the country. Women and men, except for Theo, failed him, always would fail him.

It was at Nuenen, where his father was now pastor, that in 1885 his period of bleak realism culminated in that amazing, awesome work *The Potato Eaters*; it was the sum total of all he had learned in his years of drawing workers. From that point onwards it was blazing colour that would carry his work to its heights. His physical travels were to be very limited; Antwerp, Paris, Provence his boundaries. Alone, increasingly eccentric, a law unto himself, he forsook the cold Nordic greyness of his early work and sought the south, its radiant colour, light and warmth.

> I have never before had such good fortune, nature here is *extraordinarily* beautiful. Everywhere the dome of the sky is a wonderful blue, the sun has a radiance of pale sulphur and it is sweet and charming like the combination of celestial blues and yellows in Vermeer... But I have made up my mind quite firmly not to draw another picture in charcoal.

And, painting at Saint-Rémy:

> At the moment I am working in the olive-trees, seeking the varied effects of a grey sky against a yellow earth, with the black-green of the foliage; another time, the earth and foliage all violet against a yellow sky; then a red ochre earth and green-pink sky... I am still devouring nature. Sometimes I exaggerate and change the motif; but I do not invent the whole of the picture, on the contrary I find it ready made, but it needs to be unravelled from nature.

At Arles, transported by this new vision he had received, he wrote:

> What strikes me here, and what makes painting alluring for me here, is the transparency of the air;

you cannot imagine what it is like... At an hour's distance one can distinguish the colours of things: the grey-green of the olive-trees, the green of the grass in the meadows for example, and the lilac-pink of a ploughed field... I work even in the full mid-day sun, without any shade, in the fields of corn, and I am enjoying it like a grasshopper.

When he went to France he not only began to paint like a Frenchman; he virtually became the Frenchman which many people now automatically assume him to have been. In Holland, in the colder Northern light, the flat landscape and the absence of luxuriousness of Nature or of life, he had learnt to draw, had developed his geometry and draughtsmanship and habit of working out of doors. His subjects were drab peasants at colourless toil, the only parts of the monotonous landscape actually capable of motion.

His short time in Belgium was a buffer period for him, a time of transition when he discovered colour, through the Rubens portraits he studied in galleries and the Japanese prints he began to collect. He also began that remarkable series of self-portraits - some forty of them in all, more than any other major artist has left us - which show us so much of his inner as well as outer self.

But it was when he reached France that his art blossomed out like one of his own flowers; as though he represented a bulb brought from the damp Dutch earth and exposed to the bright warm light. Émile Bernard put it expressively in the preface to the 1911 edition of Vincent's letters to him:

Everything about him as a Dutchman was opposed to that very conquest he strove for. Through the Impressionists, with their free imagination and relaxed lyricism, he would find a better way for himself... 'We are working towards the French Renaissance,' he wrote to his brother Theo (who, at his urging, exhibited Monet at the Boussod-Valadon Gallery) 'and I feel more French than ever at this task; here we are in a motherland.' And it was true, Vincent was becoming French: he painted Montmartre, its stunted little gardens, the Moulin de la Galette, its taverns; he even took excursions as far as Asnières. He visited the island of La Grande Jatte, already becoming known for Seurat's schematic researches there. Setting out with a large canvas slung on his back, he would then divide it up into compartments, according to the varied subjects he came across. In the evening he brought it back full, like some itinerant museum in which all the impressions of the day were caught. There were glimpses of the Seine full of boats, and islets with blue seesaws, neat little restaurants with their multicolour blinds amid oleanders, corners of neglected gardens, or houses for sale.

His art thawed and galvanised him. He seized impressions as he came upon them and thrust them on to canvas with more and more impatient technique before they could escape him. He worked always from his subject where he found it, never from notes or memory in a studio. His intensity and impatience gave him a frightening aspect and manner towards other human beings, thereby lessening the chances of attaining the understanding and love he so longed to receive and return. He realised that he was 'a man of passions, capable of and subject to doing more or less foolish things, which I happen to repent more or less, afterwards.' He knew that it could only lead to misunderstanding and rejection, but there was nothing he could do about it.

It was anything but self-admiration which caused him to make all those self-portraits. He was constantly watching himself, in all his changes of mood and states. 'I would rather paint the eyes of men than cathedrals,' he wrote, and the eyes in those portraits tell his story. It is one of rejection. He had been at odds with his father, spurned by the girls he had taken for granted would return the love he offered them, found wanting by the Church he had aspired to serve, unable to maintain the relationship with Paul Gauguin on which he had placed so many hopes and prepared the way for with such pathetic eagerness, and endlessly denied his dream of creating an artists' brotherhood.

It can be no coincidence that his rapid deterioration at the end coincided with the prospect of losing his one fixed certainty in human relationship, the wholehearted love and support of his dearest friend, his brother. Theo's marriage, his fatherhood, his declining financial standing must have struck successive blows at what little security Vincent felt; not only because he saw his allowance jeopardised, but because Theo's chief concern was step by step becoming pledged to others. It was the last, intolerable rejection.

One would like to leave him in the happy South, learning and painting, growing old in as much contentment as his restless spirit would ever find. The story of Vincent is as short as it is sad, an account of his life inconsiderable beside the volume of work he left, his rich gift to the world. Somewhere in his wonderful letters he tells Theo, 'Carlyle rightly says, Blessed is he who has found his work.'

That he certainly did, for all his sufferings. The last words he wrote, in a note left in his pocket for Theo, were: 'We can only make our pictures speak.'

Michael and Mollie Hardwick

Turbulent Youth

1853 – 1876

VINCENT VAN GOGH, one of the most extraordinary figures in the history of art, came like many another genius from a wholly unremarkable background. Among his ancestors had been preachers, consuls, goldsmiths, and one sculptor. His father, Theodorus van Gogh, was Protestant pastor at the village of Groot Zundert in North Brabant in the south of Holland, near the Belgian border. All four of the parishes he was to hold in his life were to be in this region.

In May 1851 Theodorus married Anna Cornelia Carbentus, six years his senior, born on 10 September 1819 and thus thirty-three years old when she gave birth to her first child on 30 March 1852. The baby was still-born. Christened Vincent Willem, he was buried in the graveyard of the village church. The death was a terrible blow to the couple, but when, exactly a year later, Anna van Gogh gave birth to a second boy, they called him Vincent Willem also. Superstitious folk might have thought it a dangerous thing to risk, and by a curious coincidence both children were registered under the same number, 29, a fact which has been made much of by some biographers, suggesting that the young Vincent must have felt himself to be walking in the place which should have been another's. Vincent was certainly 'conceived in sadness', and his mind must have been impressed whenever he went to church and passed a gravestone bearing his own name and with a date of birth only differing from his by a year.

Anna van Gogh had five more children. These were Anna Cornelia, Theodorus (the Theo who was to be Vincent's closest friend and staunchest supporter), Elizabeth Huberta, Cornelis Vincent and Wilhelmien Jacoba. Vincent appears to have had much more in common with his mother than with his father, a kind enough man, loved by his parishioners but lacking intellectual rigour and ambition. His mother had a stronger personality with greater self-possession. She had some talent as a water colourist and botanist, whose love of nature was expressed in charming needlework designs and delicate flower studies.

Vincent, too, showed an aptitude for sketching and modelling, and made a hobby of natural history, collecting beetles and empty birds' nests, which seemed to fascinate him. Although it embarrassed him to hear his drawings praised, they revealed accomplishments rare in one so young, not merely competent but demonstrating an intensity of visual perception. That quality was to remain with him throughout his life, so that it is possible to compare his early studies of flowers with those he was to produce in his last Saint-Rémy days, and to compare these latter in turn with works by expert botanists.

During 1861, Vincent began to attend the local parish school. He was red-haired, blue-eyed and freckle-faced, yet already with a strangely melancholic look. After a time, his parents began to consider the school inadequate for him and felt he was growing too 'rough', and on 1 October 1864 he was sent to a Protestant boarding-school, fifteen miles away at Zevenbergen. The change brought no startling academic improvement; during his two years there he remained nothing more than an 'average' pupil, of adequate behaviour. He spent a further unexceptional eighteen months receiving higher education at Tilburg. Perhaps the single positive acquisition from this was an unquenchable appetite for books, especially stories of the poor and persecuted, such as *Uncle Tom's Cabin*.

On leaving school he spent fifteen months at home before, in July 1869, at the age of sixteen, he was sent to The Hague, where his Uncle Cent (abbreviated from Vincent) had got him a position. Uncle Cent had made a success as an art dealer and had sold his business to the firm of Goupil & Co, which sold original works and well-produced reproductions in its galleries in Paris and branches in Brussels, Berlin and London. Vincent's job at the Hague branch was as a clerk, but the nature of the merchandise quickly made its impression on him and he was soon visiting galleries and museums, widening his knowledge of art in general.

At the beginning of 1871 the van Gogh family left Zundert for Helvoirt, where Theodorus had been appointed pastor. The following year, after Vincent had been working at The Hague for three years, he received a visit from his brother Theo. It was to be a meeting of tremendous importance for both of them. Vincent was nineteen and Theo fifteen, but their friendship immediately became so great that they swore to remain true to it and always to keep in touch, come what may. Theo was at school at Oisterwijk, and soon they began to exchange letters, beginning the remarkable correspondence without which so little would be known or understood of the complex being that was Vincent van Gogh.

Theo devotedly preserved 661 of Vincent's letters, while only a few of Theo's to Vincent survive. Vincent's letters provide us with a detailed autobiography and record of his thoughts and preoccupations, with occasional gaps where the correspondence lapsed temporarily. Many of the letters are very long, some referring to his practical work and others intimate and self-analytical. Yet at all times they are immensely revealing and articulate, worthy of comparison, in the opinion of the critic Meyer Shapiro, with the works of great introspective Russian authors.

On 13 June 1873 Vincent was sent to work at Goupil's branch in London. He was twenty years old. He donned a top hat, which he rightly felt everyone should wear in London, and highly incongruous it must have looked on him. He enjoyed the city and its museums and art galleries immensely and grasped the opportunity to improve his English, although he was homesick for Holland. He lived much as he had in The Hague and enjoyed the work, at which he was making a success for himself, managing to keep up some drawing in his spare time. His lodgings were adequate, but they were some distance from Goupil's in the Strand, so in August he left them and became a lodger at the home of Mrs Loyer, the wife of a French emigré. It turned out to be more than just a change of abode; before long he had fallen hopelessly in love with his landlady's daughter.

Eugénie (not Ursula as some have recorded) ran a day-school for children with her mother. Vincent, who had only his small wages, had to hope for rapid promotion in order to be able to marry. A further problem was that, convinced by the strength of his own passion that Eugénie's could scarcely be less, he had not yet broached the subject to her. Several months were allowed to pass before, on the eve of returning to Holland for his summer holiday, he declared his love. Eugénie's response was shattering: she not only felt no love for him, but was engaged to one of her mother's previous lodgers.

The rejection was a terrible blow to him. He needed to love, and had never imagined that his love might not be returned. His parents were so worried by the strange semi-religious tone which his letters began to take on that they asked one of his uncles to visit him and report on his state. He found nothing encouraging to report. After a miserable holiday, Vincent had, not surprisingly, given up the London lodgings associated with his heartache, and found new ones. His despair was undiminished, however; he withdrew further into himself. His worried parents turned again to Uncle Cent for help. It was forthcoming, and in October 1874 Vincent was transferred to the firm's head office in Paris.

The move achieved nothing. At the end of December he returned to London for another five months of solitary brooding and Bible reading. He showed marked loss of interest in his job, and his behaviour began to annoy his employers, who transferred him back to Paris against his will. Whenever he was not at work, he would be found reading the Bible aloud together with a fellow employee, Harry Gladwell, the eighteen-year-old son of a London art dealer, also religious-minded, though less fanatically so than his Dutch colleague. Ironically, they were lodging in Montmartre, a district not much noted for piety among its young men. Vincent further displeased his employers by taking to criticising their wares in the hearing of customers. When he visited his parents that Christmas at Etten, where his father had become pastor, they found it necessary to discuss his employment. The concern was no longer for him alone, but about the danger of his behaviour beginning to reflect on his Uncle Cent's judgement in getting him his place. Also, his brother Theo had joined the Brussels branch of Goupil's at the beginning of 1873, and was making an excellent impression.

Only Theo appears to have recognised that Vincent might make a career as an artist. Despite his interest in the Bible, Vincent had paid no less attention to art and continued to visit museums and cover his walls in engravings. He particularly admired the Barbizon school of painters, Millet in particular, but had yet to discover the Impressionists.

On his return to Paris, Vincent was told that he would be required to leave Goupil's on 1 April 1876. He was quite unperturbed and wrote to Theo, 'When the apple is ripe, a soft breeze makes it fall from the tree.'

25

Searching and Suffering

1876 – 1880

MUCH HAS BEEN MADE of what commentators feel
to have been failures in van Gogh's life. Superfici-
ally, however, he seems to have been quite un-
affected by his 'failure' to hold on to a steady job at
Goupil's. What is certain is that this break with the
art dealers represented an irrevocable break with
his past. But he was never one to avoid confrontation, nor to sit idly by and allow fate to run its
course. Evidently still hoping that he could persuade Eugénie Loyer to change her mind, his
sights remained on England; from January 1876
onwards he scanned the English newspapers in the
hope of finding a suitable job advertised there, pre-
ferably as a teacher. As yet, he seems to have conceived no definite ambition to become an artist.

Just in time, on 4 April, he received a letter from
a schoolmaster in Ramsgate offering him one
month's unpaid trial. He wrote delightedly to Theo,
'At all events I shall have board and lodging free.'
He arrived at William Stokes's school on the afternoon of 17 April, only to find that Mr Stokes himself was away in London. He was shown round the
small boarding establishment, set on the sea front
with a fine view which was to offer him tranquil inspiration for the short time he was to remain there,
teaching French, German and mathematics. There
was not much else to trouble him; only twenty-four
boys attended the school. After a few weeks there
he informed Theo that he intended to walk to

London, where he would see Harry Gladwell and various other friends, though it is likely that the thought of Eugénie there had something to do with the undertaking. He stayed two days in London before pressing on to Welwyn in Hertfordshire, where his sister Anna had been teaching French for some months.

As always, Vincent's conscience guided his actions. His love of the Church remained with him and what was later to become his missionary zeal provoked him to write to Theo, after passing once again through London, 'There is such a longing for religion among people in the large cities.' His own longing for religion in his life was intense, combined with a growing desire to sacrifice himself for others.

Mr Stokes had removed his boarding school to Isleworth, on the Thames, where Vincent continued to teach for a couple of weeks, although the schoolmaster had informed him that he could not afford to pay him; he could get teachers easily enough for only their board and lodging. But on 1 July Vincent believed that he had found the answer to his need to serve when he was engaged as a kind of curate by a Methodist minister, named Jones, at Isleworth. He must have felt that he had now found his vocation following in the footsteps of three generations of van Goghs who had become pastors, triumphantly reporting home when he was asked to preach a sermon. His depressions vanished: he began to visit the poor, comfort and teach the sick. Each Sunday he was given the opportunity to preach in the Methodist chapels of Petersham and Turnham Green, but more and more his conscience drew him to consider the plight of the poverty-stricken in the East End of London. He was well acquainted with the novels of George Eliot and Charles Dickens, and their depictions of misery urged him all the more to devote himself to the underprivileged. His work at the school seemed irrelevant by comparison. At the end of the year he returned once more to Holland to spend Christmas at Etten with his whole family and contemplate his future.

It was agreed among them that his modest salary

was insufficient in itself to justify his return to England. He seemed well on the road to recovery, if not entirely recovered, from his passion for Eugénie Loyer. If he were to stay in Holland, as he now proposed, he could be near his family and perhaps be of some help to his father in his ministry.

Once again it was Uncle Cent, probably with a view towards doing a good turn to both his brother and nephew, who put Vincent in the way of a new career, working for a bookseller in Dordrecht, for which his love of reading seemed to give him some qualification.

In the New Year of 1877 he took lodgings with the Rijken family there, in Tolbrugstraatje. His behaviour was still eccentric, his dramatic changes of mood provoking his fellow lodgers to taunt him; but he knew he was different from others, and had come to terms with it. He kept himself to himself, spending much of his time drawing and translating the Bible into Dutch, French, German and English simultaneously. He had no interest in the book trade and soon became bored with the routine. On Sundays he went to three, sometimes four services of various denominations and would stay up until all hours, reading, drawing, or simply pacing his room, to the irritation of his landlord, who later recalled, 'Occasionally, it was as if the fellow was out of his mind.' It was neither the first nor would it be the last time that Vincent's behaviour would provoke such speculation.

His greatest wish was to preach the Gospel, but he kept it a secret from his parents for months. He had confided, however, in a young schoolteacher friend at Dordrecht, named Görlitz, who stayed one night with the van Goghs at Etten and told them the reason for Vincent's present unhappiness.

Once again the family went into council over him. They decided he should go to Amsterdam, to study for the state examination which could enable him to study theology at university. He could stay with his Uncle Jan (Johannes), who held the rank of Vice-Admiral and was commander of the naval dockyard.

On 9 May 1877 Vincent duly arrived in Amsterdam. At twenty-four he was a little old to begin the rigorous study of Greek and Latin which was necessary preparation for what he clearly saw as a passionate commitment to the way of God. Dr M.B. Mendes da Costa, a fine classical scholar only a few years older than Vincent, was engaged to help him, and the two were soon good friends. Also, he had plenty of relatives in Amsterdam, and therefore little cause to feel the loneliness that he had known in Paris and London.

At first all went well, but soon Vincent's determination to succeed at his studies took a masochistic turn. If he felt his concentration failing he beat himself. He regularly and deliberately got himself locked out of his uncle's house and was forced to sleep in a shed without any protection. Not unnaturally, his tutor disapproved of this self-imposed penitence. His displeasure merely added to Vincent's burden of melancholy and despair, and he would turn up for his lessons with a bunch of snowdrops in order to placate da Costa. 'Mendes', as Vincent called him, found it hard to be angry with the strange-looking young man who, to his brother Theo's mind, somewhat resembled Rodin's depiction of John the Baptist.

It was soon obvious, however, that Vincent was never going to be able to complete his studies or hope to pass the examinations. He was not of the frame of mind to devote himself to Greek and Latin. In an article written in 1910 and often quoted, da Costa recalled Vincent objecting to having to study languages that were no longer spoken: 'Mendes, do you seriously believe that such horrors are indispensable to a man who wants to do what I want to do: give peace to poor creatures and reconcile them to their existence here on earth?' At least one commentator, Marc Edo Tralbaut, has argued, however, that it is a mistake to accept that Vincent was simply too old (in his twenties) or incapable of studying enough to pass his examinations, pointing to his undoubted intelligence and his having been already fluent and widely read in at least four other languages. When it came to a far more demanding task than learning examination Latin and Greek - establishing himself as a master artist - he applied himself and attained the greatest heights.

The likeliest explanation of what van Gogh himself termed his 'failure' is that his interest in art, as yet unrealised in its fullness, was part and parcel of the 'repressed ambition' which was waiting to burst forth, but had not yet found its vent. Shortly after his arrival in Amsterdam he had written to Theo: 'A great deal of study is needed for the work of men like Father, Uncle Stricker (who was also a pastor) and so many others, just as for painting.' He was closer to a great truth than he realised.

In July 1878 Vincent gave up his studies in Amsterdam and followed his ambition to become a missionary. Nonetheless, he was still required to undergo some training in order to be accepted. Together with his father and Mr Jones of Isleworth, who was visiting Etten, he set off for a training establishment at Laeken near Brussels; fortunately, knowledge of the classics was only a minor requirement. He spent a month preparing for admission to the school, at the same time beginning to study the work of Rembrandt and other painters. Only his mother recognised anything like the truth - that much as it appealed to him to qualify for missionary work among the poor of Belgium, his temperament would not let him settle down to study for it. He started at the school on 25 August, on a three-month probationary period. His mother was not mistaken: on being asked during a grammar lesson whether a word was nominative or dative, he replied, 'Oh, sir, I really don't care!'

The Committee of Evangelisation refused to pass him, and once again he despaired. His father took the first train to Brussels, to encourage him not to give up hope. He found his son weak, thin, sleepless and nervous. If only he wouldn't insist always on choosing the most difficult path; though the school authorities were more inclined to put it down to plain eccentricity. As a compromise, it was agreed that Vincent could go to the Borinage mining district in the south of Belgium, near Mons, at his own expense. He would work as an evangelist, giving bible classes and visiting the poor.

He set out on 26 December 1878. He found the

Borinage a bleak land of poverty, open-cast mines and giant slag heaps. He lodged with a pedlar named van der Hagen, duly tended the sick and gave lessons and bible readings. The miners' living conditions were distressing, to say the least, and the landscape satanic, but Vincent was not to be perturbed. Once again, he felt that he had found his purpose in life.

'Most of the miners are thin and pale from fever,' he wrote to Theo; 'they look tired and emaciated, weather-beaten and aged before their time. On the whole the women are faded and worn. Around the mine are poor miners' huts, a few dead trees black from smoke, thorn hedges, dung hills, ash dumps, heaps of useless coal, etc.' A miner who had worked at one pit for thirty-three years took him more than two thousand feet underground, past levels which had already been exhausted to others where the miners were working in cells so small that they were compelled to wield their picks lying down. Children loaded the coal into carts which were pulled up to the surface on rails by horses. 'The villages here look desolate and dead and forsaken; life goes on underground instead of above. One might live for years and never know the real state of things unless one went down in the mines.' It was typical of Vincent that he should try to gain an intimate understanding of the people he was to work among.

The mission authorities had promised his father that his son would be given a temporary post from January 1879, and he was sent to Wasmes for a trial period, on fifty Belgian francs a month. Vincent understood that it was deeds and not words that would bring relief, if any were possible, to the people of the Borinage. He exchanged his new lodgings with a baker's family for a hovel, where he slept on straw. He gave away all he had - his money, clothes and bed - and lived on bread and water. His superiors were quick to reprimand him for such excess of zeal and self-denial; he heeded their words at first, but soon returned to his former ways. Some have seen his behaviour as the result of a naive and over-literal interpretation of the Bible. It seems more likely that it was instinctive desire to become intimate with their suffering, that was to remain with him long after he had become disillusioned with the Church.

His understanding mother lamented wistfully, 'He does not comply with the wishes of the committee and nothing will change him. It seems that he is deaf to all remarks that are made to him.' The committee shared that view, and when his six-month probationary period ended in July he was dismissed.

Once more he faced his 'failure' head-on and walked to Brussels to see one of the clergymen who had been on the committee which had originally accepted him for training. Mr Pietersen proved sympathetic; he shared the young man's love of art. He showed interest in Vincent's drawings, and suggested that he continue his work in the Borinage without the assistance, or at least financial support, of the Church.

The following month, August 1879, Vincent moved to Cuesmes, where he lodged in a house which was shared by an evangelist and a miner and his family. He was appalled by the living and working conditions and the rates of pay, and immediately went to express his views to the mine bosses. As anyone more worldly could have predicted, they laughed at him, threatening to have him shut up in a madhouse if he did not leave them alone. He recognised that they were not given to idle threats. When, shortly afterwards, there was a strike, and the miners were preparing to set fire to one of the mines, Vincent persuaded them that violence would achieve nothing against such men.

He himself was living in dire poverty, giving away what little money Theo sent him, existing off crusts and often not eating for days on end. Theo, the only person likely to make him see reason, was sent to the Borinage to see what might be done. Vincent expressed ungrateful hurt at his criticisms and only withdrew further into himself. For nine months he declined to write to his family, even to Theo. Nothing is known of what he went through during this period, let alone how he managed to survive, apparently without enough food or clothes. When he did emerge from his silence he likened his period of withdrawal to a bird's moulting time. It was not, he assured Theo in his letter, something to be done in public, nor was it at all amusing. The only course was to hide oneself. But, he admitted, he had been homesick.

During the winter of 1880, with ten francs in his pocket, Vincent had set off to visit the French painter Jules Breton, who had built a new studio at Courrières, some thirty-five miles away. Vincent had much admired Breton's work, and was eager to see him. It took him nearly a week to get there, but when he arrived he found that the building was of modern brick 'with a Methodist regularity, an inhospitable, chilly and irritating aspect.' He went home again without so much as knocking on the painter's door. His period of 'moulting' had followed this experience. Exhausted and depressed though it left him, he was at last certain what his future was to be:

> Even in that deep misery I felt my energy revive, and I said to myself, In spite of everything I shall rise again: I will take up my pencil which I have forsaken in my discouragement and I will go on with my drawing. From that moment everything has seemed transformed to me.

Vincent van Gogh had at last discovered his true vocation. He was reborn. 'I look at things with different eyes than I did before I began to draw.'

He set about studying drawing, in the hope of making something 'presentable and saleable as soon as possible', beginning with simple exercises which he found in a manual, and made copies from engravings after Millet, an artist he had long admired and would continue to admire for the rest of his life.

It was August 1880, and Vincent had less than ten years of that life left in which to complete the enormous task he had set himself.

Love, Passion and Art

1880 – 1883

SO IT WAS that at the age of twenty-seven Vincent van Gogh embarked on one of the most difficult careers man can challenge himself with - that of an artist. In October 1880, feeling cramped by his limited working conditions in the Borinage, he finally moved to Brussels where he stayed at the cheapest hotel he could find. The light in the room of the cottage where he stayed in the Borinage had been too poor even to draw by; he found 72 Boulevard du Midi a great improvement, and soon came to the decision that he needed a model.

As usual, it was Theo who was able to give practical and moral help. He kept his brother supplied with money, encouraged him in whatever he chose to do, and got him introductions to other artists. Their advice to Vincent was to get himself properly trained. Encouraged by the fact that it would be free of charge, he applied for enrolment at the Academy in Brussels, rather than go to Amsterdam.

While waiting for a reply he studied furiously. He spent almost all his waking hours studying drawing from a book of anatomy and copying from prints, such as Millet's *The Diggers* and *The Woodcutter*, which Theo sent him. Virtually every penny was spent on his lodgings and what passed for board - bread and a cup of coffee three times a day. 'My chief food,' he wrote to Theo, 'is dry bread and some potatoes or chestnuts which people sell here on the street corners.' He assured Theo, however, that he occasionally took a meal in a restaurant in order to sustain himself properly. Whether he ever did so is doubtful; he only ever seemed capable of worrying about his health after the damage caused by self- neglect had been done.

The modern biographer Tralbaut states that Vincent was registered at the Academy in Brussels on 15 September 1880, though Johanna van Gogh Bonger, who became Theo's wife, said categorically that he was never admitted. It is a minor point, however, as it is clear that the academic training offered would never have appealed to him, nor would he have been likely to have benefited from it, whatever his fellow artists in Brussels had told him. Another of Theo's introductions was to prove much more significant.

Anthon G.A. Ridder van Rappard was a welltodo young man studying art in Brussels. He lived in comparative luxury in a large studio, where Vincent became a frequent visitor. Despite their very different circumstances, and van Rappard's initial apprehension at Vincent's appearance and extraordinary behaviour, the two soon became good friends. Here at last was someone with whom Vincent could discuss what obsessed him most. The friendship was to last five years, ending not as a result of Vincent's behaviour, but because of van Rappard's extraordinary insensitivity in attacking a painting of his that he had worked on for an unusually long time. His criticisms were not wholly unfounded, but the manner in which they were expressed was unnecessarily crude and hurtful. Van Rappard seems always to have remembered Vincent with affection; after his death he wrote to his mother:

> I remember as if it happened yesterday the moment of our first meeting in Brussels when he came into my room at nine o'clock in the morning, how at first we did not get on very well together, but so much better after we had worked together a few times... whoever had

witnessed this wrestling, struggling and sorrowful existence could not but feel sympathy for the man who demanded so much of himself that it ruined his body and mind. He belonged to the breed that produces great artists.

While Vincent's stay in Brussels was productive enough, after five months there was little to be gained by lingering there. He had heard that Theo was to be returning to Etten for Easter, and wrote to tell him that he would be there too. Van Rappard was returning to Holland and Vincent would miss his stimulating company. Furthermore, he was feeling the limitations of his own room as a place suited to working as well as living. He was prohibited from attaching prints and drawings to the walls, and the light was inadequate. There would be no shortage of subjects in his native Brabant. 'Drawing the model with the necessary costumes is the only true way to succeed,' he explained to his parents. 'Only if I study drawing thus seriously and thoroughly, always trying to portray truly what I see, shall I arrive; and then notwithstanding the inevitable expenses, I shall make a living.'

The costumes to which Vincent referred were those of the working people, such as the Brabant blue smock which he himself wore. His outlandish manner of dressing was one of the many habits which caused his parents some despair. His relationship with them had never been a settled one, but he braced himself for an effort and before departing for Etten assured Theo, 'I am willing to give in about dress or anything else to suit them.' He did manage to get on well with them this time, and with good regular meals his health improved. He spent much of his time out in the fields, drawing the peasants at work, sowing, ploughing or digging. In poor weather he worked indoors, where he made studies of the women cooking, sewing, or resting from their hard work. It was in his explorations of the countryside, however, that Vincent really found what he was seeking. His drawings of this period demonstrate an intense struggle to come to terms with the dignity of his subjects, the peasants, their homes and the landscape, and with his materials.

Considering that he had only recently begun to work seriously as an artist, many of the drawings represent undeniable technical accomplishments that were no longer wholly dependent on any striving for academic acceptance. He was searching for a form of expression which would add something new to art - an expression of the subject's essence, both external and internal. He was beginning to allow what he saw to dictate the method by which it was represented, and to set free his internal response to those subjects to express itself through them. While his work was in no way expressionistic, he was discovering the instructive relationship between the eye, the brain (or mind) and the hand. His work already had a boldness and self-assurance that was to become characteristic, but inevitably lacks the consistency of thought, study and vision which can only be attained after years of constant hard work. Despite his lack of formal training and his isolation from the artistic discourse that he knew was essential to him, Vincent was remarkably aware of the progress he had made and of the immensity of the tasks ahead.

> I have learned to measure and to observe and to seek for broad lines. So what seemed to be impossible before is gradually becoming possible now, thank God. I have drawn five times over a man with a spade, a digger in different positions, a sower twice, a girl with a broom twice. Then a woman in a white cap, peeling potatoes; a shepherd leaning on his staff; and, finally, an old, sick farmer sitting on a chair near the hearth, his head in his hands and his elbows on his knees. And of course I shall not stop here - when a few sheep have crossed the bridge, the whole flock follows. Diggers, sowers, ploughers, male and female, they are what I must draw continually. I have to observe and draw everything that belongs to country life - like many others

have done before, and are doing now. I no
longer stand helpless before nature, as I used
to... The drawings I have done lately have little
resemblance to those I used to do.

It was another promise that Vincent was to keep:
he was to remain as devoted to these subjects as he
would to his brother Theo.

He worked hard throughout the spring. When
his parents invited van Rappard to come and stay
the two friends continued their working relationship. The experience was an important one for
Vincent, who in years to come was to find such
companionships with other artists essential to his
ambition. As he told his friend Eugéne Boch on
hearing that he and his sister had begun to work
together, 'I think it is a very pleasant thing for you
to be working in the same house.'

In the early summer another visitor arrived
from Amsterdam to stay at the presbytery. Her
name was Kee Vos, a cousin of Vincent's on his
mother's side. Like both their mothers, Kee had
married a pastor. He had recently died, leaving
her widowed with a four-year old son, and she had
come to Etten in the hope that its peace and quiet
would aid her recovery from her grief. Vincent
was sincerely touched by her sorrow and quickly
made close friends with her and her son, the three
of them taking long walks together. Kee was glad
to have a companion who was sympathetic to her
unhappiness and loneliness. Her obvious grati-
tude, however, led Vincent into believing that the
love which he was soon feeling for her was
mutual. It was his second mistake of that kind:
she was quite unaware of his feelings, regarding
him merely as a kindly, if eccentric, relative.
When he finally told her of his love her reply
could not have been firmer: 'No, no, never.'

As on that previous occasion he found himself
incapable of taking the rejection as final. He felt
he must pursue the course that his heart dictated
until he had attained the object of his desire... 'for
love is something so positive, so strong, so real,
that it is impossible for one who loves to take back

39

the feeling as it is to take his own life,' he told Theo.

Kee left for her parents' house in Amsterdam almost immediately. Vincent wrote letter after letter, pleading with her to see him; they were left unopened. Kee's parents, the Strickers, and the van Goghs must have feared the worst from Vincent's fragile temper and unpredictable ways. He told Theo that he flatly refused to accept her rebuff, that his determination to win her over was boundless, and that if she should marry another man he would go far away from them all.

> Since the beginning of this love, I have felt that unless I gave myself up to it entirely, without any second thoughts, without any restriction, with all my heart, entirely and forever, there was no chance for me whatever; and even so, my chance is slight. But what is it to me whether my chance is slight or great? I mean, must I consider this when I love? No, no reckoning - one loves because one loves.

He filled his letters to Theo with justifications and proclamations of his love for Kee. It has been suggested that, in a perverse way, he enjoyed the impossibility of fulfilling his desire, in the sense that to love and not be loved in return was better than not to love at all. Be that as it may, with Kee still refusing to open his letters, let alone answer them, and Pastor Stricker remaining equally unresponsive to pleas for him to intercede, Vincent wrote to Theo declaring that there was nothing for it but to go to Amsterdam, and requesting the necessary money. He assured his brother that their parents would not oppose his going, so long as they were not to become involved. Theo, ever responsive to his wishes, sent the money.

Taking the first train to Amsterdam, Vincent went straight to the Strickers' home on the Keizersgracht. Having been told that the family was still at dinner, he waited and after a while was admitted to the dining room. Kee was not there; his aunt told him she was out. Vincent was convinced that she had only just left and that her place at the table had been quickly removed. He asked again, 'Where is Kee?' This time his uncle replied, 'Kee left the house as soon as she heard that you were here.' Months later Vincent told his brother of what followed: how he had thrust his hand into the flame of a lamp and insisted, 'Let me see her for as long as I can keep my hand in the flame.' Horrified, Uncle Stricker blew out the lamp, but remained adamant that his daughter would not appear. In the argument which followed, Uncle Stricker accused Vincent of attempting to coerce Kee. Remarkably, no tempers were lost; indeed, the Strickers offered to find Vincent lodgings for the night. 'Dear me,' he wrote to Theo, 'those two old people went with me through the cold, foggy, muddy streets and they did indeed show me a very good, cheap inn.'

He spent two more days in Amsterdam, presumably taking stock of the situation. He had a further talk with his uncle who 'muttered something about a woman's passions - I don't remember what.' Vincent had had enough of the clergy and of Amsterdam, but the prospect of returning to Etten was equally unappealing. In spite of his assurance to Theo, he had had a serious disagreement with his father before departing for Amsterdam. He had been accused of being 'indelicate' and 'untimely' in his attentions towards Kee and of damaging a family relationship, to which he had retorted, 'That is how it would be if there were no tie of affection between us; but fortunately it does exist and it will not be broken so easily. But I beg you, do not use that miserable expression "breaking family ties" again.' His furious father's own response was to curse him.

Little wonder that rather than return to Etten and let them tell him how sensibly Kee and her parents had handled him, he decided to go to The Hague. Shortly after his arrival there he called on Anton Mauve, a leading painter who had married one of Vincent's cousins. Mauve was frank with Vincent: 'I always thought you rather dull, but now I see it isn't true.' He went on to criticise some of Vincent's drawings. The young artist was delighted; here at last was a man of the world who knew something of what he was talking about. He sat Vincent down in front of a still life with clogs, gave him a set of paints and freely offered advice. It was just the style of tuition Vincent needed.

In the wake of his rejection by Kee, Vincent floundered in sore need of human companionship, I cannot, I may not live without love. I am a man, and a man with passions; I must go to a woman, otherwise I shall freeze and turn to stone.' He told Theo that he had found one, though 'not young, not beautiful, nothing remarkable.' She did not have the hands of a lady, like Kee, 'but the hands of one who works much; but she was not coarse or common, and there was something very womanly about her.' In fact, she had worked for almost half of her thirty-two years as a prostitute. When he met her she was ill, pregnant, and looking after her sick eleven-year-old daughter. Her name was Clasine Maria Hoornik, shortened by him to Sien.

But Vincent had no money to remain in The Hague and again relied on Theo to send him his fare to Etten for Christmas. This time he found himself incapable of getting on with his parents, especially his father. Their frequent quarrels came to a head on Christmas Day, when Vincent refused to go to church. Not content with this, he provoked his father by condemning the Church in general, saying 'straight out that I considered the whole system abominable.' His father was furious and shouted 'Get out of my house, the sooner the better, and rather in half an hour than an hour.' With those words the son's worship of his father was irrevocably ended, together with the interest in religion which had once been his preoccupation. His father, Pastor Stricker and the mission committee in Brussels which had rejected him had spoiled it for him between them. The passion had been replaced with a much greater one: he would give himself to painting.

Theo's response to the family split was not in the least sympathetic to his brother: 'That you could bear it no longer is possible, and that you differ in opinion with people who have lived all their lives in the country and have not come into contact with modern life is not unnatural; but, confound it, what made you so childish and impudent as to embitter and spoil Father's and Mother's life in that way?' Though largely unrepentant, Vincent did write a lengthy letter to Theo in his defence and sent a New Year's greeting to his father expressing his hope that there should be no more bitterness between them in the following year.

Back at The Hague he found himself a small studio and returned to Mauve for assistance in his studies. Mauve continued to be helpful, giving him introductions and materials, but when Vincent smashed the plaster casts that Mauve provided him to draw from, saying that he wanted to draw life and not cold plaster, Mauve began to avoid his protégé. Similarly, the advice that Vincent was given by Tersteeg, Goupil's manager at The Hague, was equally unwelcome, and Vincent began to wonder whether Mauve and Tersteeg were not in league against him. It was not to be the last time that fears of a conspiracy were to trouble him, and his later fears, indeed, were to have foundation. When he happened to meet Mauve the painter informed him 'I will certainly not come to see you, that's all over. You have a vicious character.' Tersteeg categorically refused to help him to meet other artists and even threatened that he and Mauve would see to it that Vincent received no more money from Theo.

The arrogant behaviour of Mauve and Tersteeg may have had something to do with a suspicion that Vincent was hiding something from them. It may have been connected with his relationship with Sien, about which he was unrepentant: 'Nobody cared for her or wanted her, she was alone and forsaken like a worthless rag, and I have taken her up and have given her all the love, all the tenderness, all the care that was in me; she has felt this and she has revived, or rather is reviving.'

Commentators have looked for literary precedent for Vincent's attitude, sentimental love for a degraded woman, suggesting that it owed something to the works of Zola and George Eliot. 'It seems to me,' he wrote, 'that every man worth a straw would have done the same in such a case. What I did was so simple and natural that I thought I could keep it to myself.' At any rate, he was happy again for a while. He made drawings of Sien that are so firm in their line, yet so delicate and sensitive in their touch, that the power of conviction they carry must strike to the heart of even the most uninterested viewer. One notable drawing of her sitting naked in profile, bent almost double, with her head in her arms resting on her knees, is entitled simply *Sorrow*. From it Vincent drew one of the few lithographs he was ever to make.

There was a further reason for his buoyancy during the early part of this stay in The Hague; he had been given a commission for twelve drawings of the town by his Uncle Cor, who was an art dealer there. 'OM's order is like a ray of hope to me,' wrote Vincent. At last he seemed about to make some money from his work. Perhaps he would even be able to marry Sien and take care of her family.

On 7 June Vincent was admitted to hospital suffering from 'what they call the "clap", but only a mild case'. He made light of the gonorrhea, but feared that his parents might take advantage of his being in hospital to separate him from Sien for good. He need have had no fear; they sent him a package of clothes, cigars and ten guilders, and a few days later his father visited him briefly in the hospital.

Shortly afterwards it was Sien's turn to be admitted to hospital, where she gave birth to a healthy boy. Vincent was overjoyed and while she remained at the hospital recovering found a larger studio and room for them all to live in. On her arrival there, however, she seemed changed; and his pleasure was additionally shattered when Tersteeg once again began to interfere, criticising Vincent's living arrangements and giving him cause to fear a plot to declare him insane in order to get him away from Sien.

But he was soon totally absorbed again in his painting, as usual working out of doors for much of the time. He began to consider establishing a brotherhood of artists, whose work would be 'drawn from the people for the people and distributed to them in popular editions'. Though Vincent made a few lithographs and one etching in his career, he was never to put his plan into operation. The representations of his work which since his death have proved more widely popular than those of any other artist are reproductions of paintings, not works specifically designed for printing.

Theo was now supplying his brother with 150 francs each month, out of which Vincent was managing to provide for four people, as well as covering the rent and his expenses for materials and models. In August Theo visited The Hague with a warning: he could not support him *and* his dependants; he advised him to leave Sien for his own sake. Vincent would not be persuaded; all that he had managed to do for Sien would be destroyed the instant that she was compelled to seek work as a prostitute. His hopes of a settled family life with her had been fading for some time, though, and in subsequent letters to Theo he mentioned her less and less.

Theo paid him a second visit in the summer of 1883 and found him much less reluctant to leave the woman to whom, however, he was still deeply attached. Vincent was beginning to think of moving to the country once again. He had had enough of the city, and his relationship with Sien had become embittered, from disruption by her mother, who wanted her to return to steady employment, i.e. the brothel. Vincent had earned only sixty guilders over the past two years, to supplement his allowance from Theo. As usual, he blamed his own inadequacies for the situation. Some relief seemed to offer itself when his old friend van Rappard paid a visit and excited him with talk of the possible founding of an artists' colony at Drenthe, in the north of Holland. They might live under better circumstances there; but Sien was not interested. She had no desire to move to the country, and began to annoy Vincent with her ingratitude, although he remained as forbearing as ever. 'I do not think her bad,' he told Theo; 'she has never seen what is good, how can she be good?'

Nevertheless, he knew that their time together was coming to its end. He made some efforts to find her respectable work before taking himself off to Drenthe.

When Vincent finally took the train to the north, on 11 September 1883, Sien and her children came with him to the station. Parting from ones he had loved, perhaps still loved, was a deeply distressing experience and thoughts of Sien remained with him for long after. Though she outlived him, her life can have been no less a torment than his own. She returned eventually to a brothel, and was found drowned on 12 November 1904.

Vincent's stay in the Drenthe region was a short one, but the landscape, with its peat fields, mud cottages, and long canals fading into the horizon, he found magnificent. He wandered the bleak countryside drawing and painting, until within a fortnight old worries again began to torment him. He decided to take a journey on a canal peat boat to Niew-Amsterdam, where he put up at a small hotel. He had heard that the German artist Max Liebermann was staying at Zweeloo and he set out to visit the ancient village. Vincent enjoyed the winter journey by open cart and wrote a richly detailed account of it to his brother; but when he reached his destination he found that Liebermann was no longer there and was told that no painters ever came at this time of year.

As Gauguin was later to remark, winter was never a good period for van Gogh. He soon began to feel lonely, despite his pleasure in being close to the rich soil of Drenthe. He had hoped Theo would come and join him there, as he was having difficulties with his superiors at Goupil's. Vincent suggested that he too become an artist, but Theo knew himself (not to mention the art world) too well - he would remain a dealer.

Lonely and anxious, Vincent decided to go

home to his parents for Christmas. His father had become pastor at Nuenen, east of Etten, in south Holland, and his errant son arrived there early in December 1833. It was two years since the quarrel which had resulted in his being ordered out of his parents' house. The time had come to try to make yet another fresh start.

New Start at Nuenen

1884 – 1885

RETURNING TO HIS PARENTS naturally presented Vincent with difficulties. Though they had done much for him over the years, and he had had hopes of following in his father's footsteps, the divisions that had separated them two years before opened afresh shortly after his return. Nevertheless, he was to remain two years in Nuenen, and it was to be a productive period for his art, but it seemed as if fate was determined to renew the beatings that Vincent had so far survived until he would be finally forced to submit.

He had not originally intended to stay long in Nuenen, but physical exhaustion, his disappointment over the artists' colony in Drenthe, and his attraction to his home country of Brabant persuaded him to extend his visit. His relations with his parents remained strained by bitter memories and his welcome home had been little more than polite. Vincent was perplexed over his future, and the family tensions made him begin to question even Theo's devotion. At first he was inclined to regard himself and Theo on one side, with their parents on the other; then he began to see differences between himself and his supposed ally, observing in a letter to Theo, 'Neither you nor I meddle with politics, but we live in the world, in society, and involuntarily ranks of people group themselves. You and I belong *somewhere*, don't we? standing either on the right or the left, whether we are conscious of it or not.' He drew a parallel with the Paris of 1848, picturing them confronting one another across the barricades, 'you before it as a soldier of the government, I behind it as a revolutionary or rebel.' He blamed his brother for advising him to leave Sien. Vincent, however, had no time to sink into despair on his return to Nuenen.

An accident served to bring him a little closer to his parents. His mother had broken her thigh in stepping off a train at Helmond, and was confined to bed. Vincent nursed her with all the attention he had shown to the sick and injured miners of the Borinage, and amused her by making drawings, which he called 'trifles'. He had rented a large room close to his parents' house which he converted into a studio, where in due course his mother was able to enjoy visiting in a wheelchair. Hard at work at his painting, and the feeling that he was being of use to his mother, kept him happy for the time being and content to stay on at Nuenen.

He had not got over his discontentment with his brother, though. His latest complaint was that Theo, as an art dealer, was in a position to sell his pictures for him, but didn't seem to be trying. 'If you do not do anything with my work, I do not cherish your protection. A *wife* you cannot give me, a *child* you cannot give me, *work* you cannot give me. Money, yes.' Theo, characteristically, achieved a diplomatic settlement. Vincent was to regard the money sent him as payment against his work. He should send Theo his pictures each month and Theo would send Vincent 150 francs.

Artistically, Vincent was already absorbed by the Brabant landscape that he loved so much and the people for whom he had such admiration. He worked with gusto and began to think of staying there permanently. Tangible encouragement was provided by a retired goldsmith named Hermans whom he met at the shop in Eindhoven where he bought his paints, and who commissioned twelve decorative panels from him. Things went along relatively quietly for a time, but with Vincent van Gogh such a state of affairs was too good to last.

For some time a neighbour by the name of Margot Begemann had been visiting his incapacitated mother. She was ten years older than Vincent, in her forties. They began taking long walks together, and, perhaps because she was 'on the shelf', she developed an obsessive love for him. For a man who believed so firmly in the efficacy of a woman's love and preferred that woman to be older than himself, he proved disappointingly reluctant and would not even take advantage of her willingness to let him make physical love to her. He found her somewhat *passé*, and likened her to a well-made violin that had been spoiled by bad repairing.

To extend that sort of metaphor, Vincent himself was no oil painting, while his dress, manner and behaviour left almost everything to be desired. As next-door neighbours to the vicarage, her family knew a great deal about his character and reputation, and one of her two sisters seems to have made a point of finding out more. Her horrified family closed ranks against any possibility of a marriage, which Vincent had shown himself at least prepared to consider.

It was all too much for Margot. On one of her walks with him she collapsed and went into spasms. Suspecting something more than a nervous attack, he asked if she had swallowed something, and got the answer he feared. At a Utrecht hospital it was confirmed that she had taken strychnine. Her life was saved, enabling her to proclaim tragically, 'I too have loved at last!' Inevitably, the respectable people of Nuenen blamed it all on Vincent.

Almost the only contact he had with other artists, apart from van Rappard's brief visit, was with local amateurs. One of them, a tanner named Anton Kerssemakers, provided in later years a revealing description of Vincent's working environment at Nuenen:

All the available hanging or standing room was filled with paintings, drawings in watercolour and in crayon: the heads of men and women

51

whose clownish turned-up noses, protruding
cheekbones and large ears were strongly accen-
tuated, the rough paws calloused and furrowed;
weavers and weaving looms, women spooling
yarn, potato planters, women busy weeding,
innumerable still lifes, certainly as many as ten
studies in oils of the little old chapel at Nuenen,
which he was so enthusiastic about that he
painted it in all seasons and in all weathers. A
great heap of ashes around the stove, which had
never known a brush or stove polish, a small
number of chairs with cane bottoms, and a cup-
board with at least thirty different birds' nests,
all kinds of mosses and plants brought along
from the moor, some stuffed birds, a spool, a
spinning wheel, a complete set of farm tools,
old caps and hats, coarse bonnets and hoods,
wooden shoes, etc.

Vincent's accompanying lifestyle was ascetic to a
degree, denying those comforts which were available to him and even a sound diet. By contrast
with his drab existence, he was deeply engaged in
the study of colour and became particularly excited by the theories of Delacroix. He had made the
acquaintance of an organist, who had agreed to
give him piano lessons, because, as Kerssemakers
later recalled, he had become interested in the relations between sounds and colours, something that
had interested artists and composers for centuries.

During the lessons van Gogh was continually
comparing the notes of the piano with Prussian
blue and dark green and dark ochre and so on,
all the way to bright cadmium-yellow, and the
good man thought he had to do with a madman,
in consequence of which he became so afraid of
him that he discontinued the lessons.

Vincent's interest in music did not altogether
disappear, though he did give up trying to learn
the piano; it is hard to picture him practising
scales and Czerny exercises. His own art was his
overriding preoccupation, and he worked at it

furiously while at Nuenen, drawing and painting and making some lithographs. As always, he worked out of doors as much as possible and worked quickly. He told Kerssemakers, who took lessons from him, 'You must set it down all at once and then leave it alone; don't be afraid and don't try to make it pretty.' One was not to be afraid of making mistakes, even in personal relationships: 'I tell you, if one wants to be active, one must not be afraid of failures!' - a direct enough response to those who are inclined to see van Gogh's life as having been determined by his fear of failure. Such an influence undoubtedly existed, but he was probably more afraid of fear itself. If he let that get the better of him his drive to discover the modes of expression that would become the essence of his art would surely dry up. Boldness was all, even at some sacrifice of strict accuracy when instinct demanded otherwise. He told Theo, 'my great longing is to learn to make those very incorrectnesses, those deviations, remodellings, changes in reality, so that they may become, yes, lies if you like - but more true than the literal truth.'

This did not imply any spirit of carefree abandon, and fits of depression continued to plague him. His father was aware that 'it would be better for him to be among people of his own profession, but we cannot dictate to him', and in a later letter told Theo, 'This morning I had a talk over things with Vincent; he was in a reasonable mood and said there was no particular reason for his being depressed. May he meet with success of some sort.'

Two days later, on 25 March 1885, Pastor van Gogh had a heart attack and died on his own threshold, aged sixty-three. Whatever emotion it stirred in Vincent, he showed little outwardly. But he wrote to Theo a little later saying 'I am still greatly under the influence of what has just happened,' and sent him a still-life group of a vase of the plant honesty and his father's pipe and tobacco pouch, following it some weeks later with a more ironic one juxtaposing an open family bible with a closed copy of one of Zola's sensational novels.

It has often been commented that Vincent's

work had therapeutic value for him. It does seem to have been the only activity that provided him with any relief from the torments he suffered throughout his life. At the time of his father's death his mind was already deeply occupied with a scheme for an ambitious group portrayal of peasants eating their frugal meal by lamplight. The result, painted quickly in April-May, was *The Potato Eaters*, often referred to as his earliest 'masterpiece'. It is a work of deep awareness of the harsh reality of manual toil and the circumstances of those whose lives are entirely governed by it, the outcome of endless studies he had been making of peasant men and women at work in the fields and at home.

> I have tried to emphasise that those people, eating their potatoes in the lamplight, have dug the earth with those very hands they are reaching out to the dish, and so it speaks of *manual labour*, and how they have honestly earned their food... It would be wrong, I think, to give a peasant picture a certain conventional gloss. If such a picture smells of bacon, smoke, potato steam - all right, that's not offensive; if a stable smells of dung - very well, that belongs to a stable; if the field has an odour of ripe corn or potatoes or of guano or manure - that's as it should be, especially for city people to appreciate. Such pictures may *teach* them something.

The Potato Eaters is an extraordinary painting and an exceptional work. Vincent was well aware that it would be criticised, and looked forward almost eagerly to scathing comments from those who would be certain to find its realism uncomfortable and offensively harsh. He did not, however, anticipate an attack on purely technical grounds by his friend Anthon van Rappard, who found many details badly executed and gave his verdict as 'superficial'. It was enough to end their friendship, although they went on corresponding for a while.

The consensus of posterity has been that *The Potato Eaters* represents a culmination of Vincent's intensive work up to that point in his career, a work of remarkably cohesive composition with a thorough understanding of chiaroscuro clearly comprehended from the work of Rembrandt and others. The deep earth palette, despite its limitations within the period in which it was painted, obviously achieved exactly the effect that he had intended. But more than that, it foreshadowed whole facets of twentieth century art, representing a watershed between his work in Holland and the lessons he was to learn in Paris and build on in Arles, Saint-Rémy and Auvers. In this sense it is probably the most academic work that Vincent ever produced, and may justly be regarded as a masterpiece. It would be misleading, however, so to uphold it, as many have been inclined to, at the expense of more important paintings and drawings of his at that same period and earlier, which culminated in this seminal work representing a summation of all that he had absorbed so far.

The many peasant studies of those five formative years had given Vincent's technique its grounding. It is a pity that only a proportion of his mass of sketches and completed drawings survive. As that winter of 1885 approached he began to feel trapped in Nuenen; he could no longer work out of doors, lacked models and had been extending his range of subjects by painting symbolic studies of birds' nests, bleak and melancholy, despite the eggs they contained. They symbolized much of the condition of his life at this time, and his uncertain hopes. He left in November for Antwerp. His mother, too, left soon afterwards. In making her preparations she contemplated the mass of material which Vincent had left behind. The easiest means of disposal was to send it to the carpenter at Breda, to salvage what materials he could and destroy the rest.

Apart from those more or less finished works which could be sold off for a few cents each in the locality of their origin, where their creator's reputation stood so low that it had only required a peasant girl to become pregnant for him to be automatically (but unjustifiably) blamed, such was their actual fate. It was a sad ending to a doleful period; and it ended with his leaving Holland for good.

The Road to the South

1885 – 1888

VINCENT HAD KNOWN for some time that art was to be his whole life henceforward. He was drawn towards Antwerp, with its great Rubens collection, and but for van Rappard's contrary advice might have gone there directly from Drenthe. He knew that he would want to work from the model if he went to Antwerp, and knew that he would not be able to afford it. A year before leaving Holland he had set himself a pragmatic task of making some thirty paintings of heads, which he hoped might raise him some money through a dealer, and this preparatory work had served to delay though he hungered for the company of other artists with whom he could discuss his own ideas and learn from theirs.

Arriving in Antwerp at last in late November, he took a room, significantly above a colour shop at 194 rue des Images (now 224 Longue rue des Images). The change of locale seemed to stimulate a need for colour and brightness in his life and he decorated his walls with Japanese prints, whose intensity of composition, strength of line and brightness amused him and were to prove influential. Since 1858, when commercial treaties had been signed between Japan, England and France, Japanese art in various forms had been coming into Europe, and by the 1880's had become highly fashionable. The two-dimensional planes of Japanese prints excited European artists

57

reared on very different techniques, and Vincent's enthusiasm for them was shared by many of his contemporaries.

It was not his first visit to Antwerp. He and Kerssemakers had made the expedition from Nuenen together to study the works of Rembrandt and Hals in the collection of the Musée d'Art Ancien. By now Vincent had fully absorbed Delacroix's theories of colour and he became greatly impressed with the works of Rubens, from whose work he gained the notion that 'colour expresses form if well applied and in harmony'. His letters to Theo from Antwerp became more and more concerned with Rubens and colour, as his own palette reflected this new preoccupation. 'I am quite carried away by his way of drawing the lines in a face with streaks of pure red,' he wrote, and though he continued painting views of the city and still-lifes he came to concentrate on portrait painting and went in search of a blonde model 'just because of Rubens. My best chance is in the figure, because there are relatively very few who do it, and I must seize the opportunity.'

There was no lack of scope in a city whose girls he found 'sometimes damned beautiful' and began to prefer to the rather worn older women whom he had favoured in the past. He had got into the habit of talking to his models while painting them in order to keep their faces animated; indeed, the activity was drawing him out of his own shell and stimulating his sense of observation.

He walked the old, narrow streets, looking eagerly about. The colourful variety of shops and cafés gave him ideas of painting signboards for them or of working for a street photographer - anything to raise money to supplement what Theo sent, most of which went on paints and canvas.

As ever, his physical wellbeing was neglected. He lived on bread and milk for days on end, partly from frugality, but also because his teeth were too rotten to chew anything more substantial. He smoked a pipe to assuage hunger pains, which in turn made him cough offensively. To cap it all, he had syphilis. Little wonder that he was writing to

Theo in December that he felt 'rather faint', and by February that he was literally worn out and overworked. He knew the risks he was running, and that state of mind has led a number of commentators to read significance in a strange picture he produced at this time, quite different from anything else of his. It shows a skull with a cigarette between its teeth, and has a bizarre tragi-comic flavour which is quite unique. Is it meant to be a joke or a gesture of defiance? Perhaps even fear, suggests Tralbaut, adding that however it may be interpreted, as a picture it is 'an example of surrealism before its time'.

He was not entirely heedless of his condition, however, reporting to Theo an Eindhoven doctor's opinion of his chances of living long enough to do all that he sensed lay within his reach:

> Well, painting is a thing that wears one out. But Dr Van Loo told me, when I went to see him shortly before I came here, that I am after all fairly strong. That I need not despair of reaching the age which is necessary for producing one's life's work. I told him that I knew of several painters who, not-withstanding all their nervousness, etc, reached the age of sixty or seventy, luckily for themselves, and that I should like to do the same.

Earlier, a doctor in Amsterdam whom he consulted without disclosing his occupation, in order to get a frank assessment of his constitution, had unconsciously gratified him by supposing him to be an ironworker. 'This is just what I have tried to change in myself,' he explained to Theo; 'when I was younger, I looked like one who was intellectually overwrought, and now I look like a bargee or an ironworker.'

In order to paint from the figure without incurring costs that he could ill afford, Vincent decided, as he had done in Brussels, to enter the Academy of Art. He succeeded in getting admitted, but it was inevitable that his eccentricities, as well as the fact that at thirty-two he was much older than the other students, would set him apart. More visibly annoying to the Acadamicians, who considered themselves his superiors by virtue of their position, was the feverish way he applied thick areas of paint, sometimes with his fingers, so that it would drip on to the floor. He neither considered nor paused, just created or tore up and began again, or attacked his drawing paper so ferociously with the rubber that he wore holes in it.

He was removed from the life class and told to draw from the antique. He complied, and even found drawing from plaster casts quite useful in its way, although strictly according to his own impetuous methods. He refused to accept the dogmatic requirement that the first stage should be an outline; he started from within his subject and worked outward. He was noisy and opinionated, and it took him an effort to pretend to be paying some heed to his tutors, in order to keep his place in the Academy and the few benefits which went with it. Confrontation finally came when a teacher criticised his copy of a cast of the Venus de Milo, making her appear less like a Greek goddess than a robust Flemish matron. 'God damn it!' he retorted. 'A woman must have hips and buttocks and a pelvis to carry a child!' He began to attend the academy less, preferring the city's two leading drawing clubs, where the atmosphere was informal and members were enabled to draw from the nude, which was only rarely possible at the starchy Academy.

Before being admitted to the Academy, Vincent had written to Theo to ask whether he might not move to Paris where they could share accommodation. Theo had by this time been made a manager of one of Goupil's two galleries in the French capital, and had his reputation to consider. He was a quiet, anonymous sort of man, 'pale, blond and melancholy', but with a keen artistic discrimination and an appreciation of modern art that had gained him the respect of painters and critics. The prospect of having his outrageous brother to live with him was alarming, to say the least. He tried to persuade him that Paris would be bad for his health, that he ought to go back to Nuenen, that the lease of his apartment would soon be expiring and that he had no firm plans for a new one - anything short of saying bluntly that Vincent would not be welcome. The more Vincent thought of moving to Paris, though, the more determined on it he became. 'You may be of the opinion,' he wrote to Theo, 'that I am an impossible character - but that's absolutely your own business. For instance, I need not care, and I am not going to. I know that there are times when you think differently and better of me... What I seek is so straightforward that in the end you cannot but give in.' Theo remained silent. 'I feel that you do not approve of my going straight to Paris, otherwise you would have answered me. And yet it is better to do it at once... In fact, we ought to have done it long ago.'

In the end Theo could delay the inevitable no longer. One day in February 1886 he received a note written hastily in black crayon that was enough to make his heart sink, momentarily at least: 'My dear Theo, don't be cross with me for arriving all at once like this; I have thought about it so much, and there is no point in wasting time. Shall be at the Louvre from midday on, or sooner if you like... So, come as soon as possible.'

Brother Vincent was in town.

Although he had spent a little time there ten years earlier, Paris in 1886 was rich new territory for a young artist to discover. Vincent knew little of the personalities and movements awaiting him; the Impressionists, the Symbolists, the Pointillists, the work of Degas, Manet, Cézanne. At the studio of a painter of grandiose historical subjects, Fernand Cormon, on the Boulevard de Clichy, Vincent met a number of other artists who were to become important as Post-Impressionists, including Henri de Toulouse-Lautrec, another student at Cormon's, who struck up a strong friendship with him that was to last until Vincent's death.

By the time Cormon closed his studio, in the summer of 1886, the scope of Vincent's palette had altered remarkably from the earth-colours that had predominated under the influence of Dutch tradition, before his move to Antwerp. Light, brightness and gaiety replaced them; he began to paint vivid interiors, flowers, friends in domestic surroundings and cafés, open landscapes - all very different from the peasant portraits and dark symbolism of his work in Holland and Belgium. He had been aware of the Impressionists for some years, but had been very much dependent for information about them on magazine articles sent him by Theo. Now he had the opportunity not only to see their work at first hand (he was originally disappointed in it), but also to meet the artists. The Impressionists had first exhibited as a group in 1874 and were by now fairly widely accepted within artistic circles. Edouard Manet, in many respects the founder of the movement, was already dead. Though Manet was not himself an Impressionist, his work had laid down some of the foundations on which Impressionism would be built. Vincent, however, did not see Manet as occupying a position of such influence as was ascribed to him by the novelist and critic Émile Zola: 'I cannot agree with Zola's conclusions, representing Manet as one who opens a new future to modern ideas of art; I consider Millet, not Manet, to be the essentially modern painter who opened a new horizon to many.' Though Vincent was never completely to lose his admiration for the work of Jean François Millet, when he was given the opportunity to inspect a number of originals he did not find that Millet's use of colour impressed him at all. He found the pictures grey, not at all like the work of the Impressionists who were beginning to exercise considerable influence on him, though the movement had by now effectively collapsed and in the final group exhibition Monet, Renoir and Sisley had declined to show anything. Only one leading figure, the patriarchal Camille Pissarro, remained, and became a strong, literally enlightening influence on Vincent.

A new artistic spirit was in the air, and Vincent was fortunate enough to have become a close friend of one who could introduce him to the new work that was being done in the city. Toulouse-Lautrec was eleven years younger than Vincent but the two men had a great deal in common. Both were largely self-taught. Both were attracted to popular entertainments and the seedier side of life; and both wished their work to reach a popular audience. The two painters quickly developed a deep admiration for one another's work and Lautrec introduced Vincent to the work of Gauguin, Seurat, Signac and others.

Theo was also able to be of direct assistance to Vincent. For some time now Theo had been collecting 'modern' paintings, and had been making occasional sales of Impressionist works, to which he was able to introduce Vincent. He owned paintings by Gauguin, Seurat, Manet, Toulouse-Lautrec and others, and near his apartment were the galleries where the Impressionists exhibited.

In June 1886 the two brothers had moved to a larger apartment on the third floor of number 54 rue Lepic in Montmartre. Theo had his own bedroom and Vincent a studio, but this was inadequate for his work and as a result he seems to have worked out of doors, as he had done for years and would continue to do until his death, both in Paris and on the outskirts, often going on painting expeditions with other artists. The environment seemed to be exactly what Vincent needed and his health soon began to recover. During the summer of 1886 Theo wrote to their mother:

> We like the new apartment very much; you would not recognise Vincent, he has changed so much, and it strikes other people more than it does me. He has undergone an important operation in his mouth, for he had lost almost all his teeth through the bad condition of his stomach. The doctor says that he has now quite recovered his health; he makes great progress in his work and has begun to have some success. He is in much better spirits than before and many people here like him... If we can continue to live together like this, I think the most difficult period is past, and he will find his way.

Vincent was aware of his improved health, and wrote that 'the French air cleans up the brain and does good - a world of good.' He was no longer inclined to have violent arguments, though his discussions with other painters remained lengthy and intense. One Sunday, however, he visited the painter and model Suzanne Valadon, who was a friend of Toulouse-Lautrec and others, and unpacked a series of canvases which he spread around the room. None of the artists present offered any comment, scarcely even drawing him into their conversation. After a while Vincent packed up his pictures and left as unobtrusively as he had arrived.

Within a few months of coming to Paris Vincent's many paintings of city views had taken on a range of colour that had never before been so broad. He painted a number of studies of the nearby Moulin de la Galette, and made frequent visits to Asnières where his young painter friend Émile Bernard was living. Vincent recognised that he needed to intensify his palette, and so 'last year I painted hardly anything but flowers in order to get accustomed to using a scale of colours other than grey - pink, soft and vivid green, light blue, violet, yellow, orange, rich red.' Vincent had been very impressed by the work of the landscape and portrait painter and superb colourist Adolphe Joseph Thomas Monticelli, who had recently died in Marseilles, and was later to write from Arles, 'I think of Monticelli terribly often here. He was a strong man - a little cracked, or rather very much so - dreaming of the sun and of love and gaiety, but always harassed by poverty - of an extremely refined taste as a colourist, a thoroughbred man of a rare race, continuing the best traditions of the past.'

Vincent never tired of experimentation if it seemed likely to help him in his search for an adequate mode of expression. In absorbing the work of the Impressionists and what were to become known as the Post-Impressionists, he did not fail to take a serious look at the work of the Pointillists and carry out some fine studies using the technique of painting in dots of two or more colours, which at a distance blend into a mass, developed by Seurat and Signac

A Japanese Dream

1888

'A LITTLE TOWN surrounded by fields all covered with yellow and purple flowers; exactly - can't you see it? - like a Japanese dream.'

On 20 February 1888 he arrived at the small town of Arles. It stands beside the River Rhône, an ancient town important at the time of Julius Caesar's invasion. Ruins and medieval relics abound there: the remains of the palace of the Emperor Constantine, a Roman theatre where the famous Venus of Arles was discovered, a fine cathedral, Roman ramparts and aqueducts.

But antiquities did not interest or inspire Vincent. He thought the famous porch of St Trophine admirable but 'cruel and monstrous', and was thankful not to be living in the age of Nero. He had come to Arles to paint nature, and he arrived there in time to see the spring.

'I'm up to my ears in work, for the trees are in blossom and I want to paint a Provençal orchard of astounding gaiety.' Of all his paintings of fruit-trees, the most dazzlingly beautiful is that of peach-trees in blossom, entitled *Souvenir de Mauve*. His sister Wilhelmien had sent him an obituary notice of his former tutor and cousin, Anton Mauve, whom Vincent remembered with affection, as he wrote to Theo:

> Something - I don't know what, took hold of me and brought a lump to my throat... I chose the best study

69

I've painted here purposely; I don't know what they'll say about it at home, but that does not matter to us; it seems to me that everything in memory of Mauve must be at once tender and very gay, and not a study in any graver key. You will see that the pink peach-trees are painted with a sort of passion.

The picture, indeed, is so alive that where he has applied his paint most thickly to represent the flowers on the branches of the tree it appears as if the canvas itself has literally blossomed. Here is his vision of Japan, blossom against a blue sky in sunshine. Once again this could not be a clearer indication of Vincent's inner state on his arrival at Arles. He was convinced that here at last he would be able to establish a community of artists. 'I have thought now and then that my blood is actually beginning to think of circulating, which is more than it ever did during the last period in Paris. I could not have stood it much longer.'

Vincent was now beyond the influence of the painters he had known in Paris, and his work soon took on a more individualistic expression than ever. Soon after his arrival, after the snow which had greeted him had cleared, he painted the drawbridge at Arles, a picture he entitled *Le Pont de Langlois* after the name of the bridge-keeper. There are many similar lifting-bridges in Holland, and it must have reminded Vincent of home. The bold blocks and lines of colour that create the effect clearly place the picture in a different category to the landscapes he had painted in Paris - 'a study in which the ground is bright orange, the grass bright green and the sky and water blue.' He painted the same bridge on several occasions, each an evocation of a feature of his native country, expressed in a manner owing much to the country of his dreams, Japan.

By now, he was applying thick paint directly on to the canvas without any preparatory drawing, though, of course, he often made drawings, sometimes of much the same subjects. He was convinced that this method was the correct way in which to develop an immediate and intuitive expression of his responses to the landscape and the people he met. This response was, however, now based on rock-hard foundations which Vincent had been exhaustively building day and night for the past eight years. But he was aware of the criticism that was likely to be directed at his work:

> I must warn you that everyone will think that I work too fast. Don't believe a word of it. Is it not emotion, the sincerity of one's feelings for nature, that drives us? And if the emotions are sometimes so strong that one works without knowing one works, when sometimes the strokes come with a continuity and a coherence like words in a speech or a letter, then one must remember that it has not always been so, and that in time to come there will be hard days, empty of inspiration.

He was equally aware that the deliberate, controlled exaggeration in his work would be mistaken for caricature, especially with regard to the portraits. He described to Theo how he intended to paint his Belgian artist friend Eugéne Boch.

> I exaggerate the fairness of the hair, I even get to orange tones, chromes and pale citron-yellow. Behind the head, instead of painting the ordinary wall of the mean room, I paint infinity, a plain background of the richest, most intense blue I can contrive, and by this simple combination of the bright head against the rich blue background, I get a mysterious effect, like a star in the depths of an azure sky.

But he still had no studio and was becoming dissatisfied with his lodging at the Hôtel-Restaurant Carvel, 30 rue Cavalerie. 'The people here are trying to take advantage of me,' he told Theo, 'so as to make me pay high for everything, on the pretext that I take up a little more room with my pictures than the other clients, who are not painters.' By the beginning of May he had found himself a

71

spacious studio and living accomodation at No.2 place Lamartine, better known as 'The Yellow House', of which he rented the right wing for fifteen francs a month. It provided him with four rooms, 'or rather two with two cabinets', and was to remain 'the studio and the storehouse for the whole campaign, as long as it lasts in the south.' Yellow was his favourite colour, and he thought of his new premises as 'the house of light', where he might be able to start a 'school of the South' by creating his artists' commune. Despite his enthusiastic feelings about the studio Vincent did not finish moving in until September, possibly because he was so busy painting and exploring the area.

In the meantime he paid a visit to Saint-Maries-de-la-Mer, where he stayed for a week during June, painting the boats at sea and on the shore and a view of the old town. He enjoyed the 'glorious strong heat' and described 'a light that for want of a better word I can only call yellow, pale sulphur yellow, pale golden citron! How lovely yellow is! And how much better I shall see the north!' During this period he painted one of his best-loved pictures, *The Sower*, which probably remains the most striking image of the heat of the sun ever produced. It is directly related to his enthusiasm for the work of Millet and carries with it a symbolic significance of which he wrote, 'I feel so strongly that it is the same with people as it is with wheat, if you are not sown into the earth to germinate there, what does it matter? In the end you are ground between the millstones to become bread.'

Not everything about the climate of Arles was pleasing, however, and Vincent complained to Theo of 'the nagging menace of the constant mistral', the wind that is 'so cool and dry that it gives you goose flesh'. Soon this nerve-nagging wind became an enemy, forcing him to drive pegs into the ground in order to secure his easel or even attach the canvas directly to the ground. 'What a picture I would make of it, if there was not this damned wind. That is the maddening thing here, no matter where you set up your easel. And that is largely why the painted studies are not so finished as the drawings; the canvas is shaking all the time.'

It was indeed at about this time that Vincent made one of his most masterful and complete drawings, now in the collection of the British Museum. Entitled *Landscape near Montmajour*, the drawing is almost an inventory of his highly evolved technique of using a reed pen and ink to give the impression of a vast range of textures across the paper, as the landscape recedes to the horizon. The expressiveness of his masterly skill with the reed pen inevitably puts one in mind not only of the drawings of Rembrandt but, equally importantly, of the great Japanese draughtsmen.

By now Vincent was preparing to receive visitors. He had come to realise that he might not be able to start the artists' co-operative that he had dreamed of for so long, but he could look forward to the day when the artists he had known in Paris would come to stay and to work with him, to benefit from the sun in the south and to talk. In the meantime, Vincent had already met a number of the 'good people of Arles' and had continued his work as a portraitist. Perhaps the most important of this work were the portraits of the Roulin family, who had befriended him shortly after his arrival at Arles: the father, *The Postman Roulin*, with his impressive beard which Vincent clearly enjoyed rendering as a mass of red spirals in one version, and Mme Roulin, his wife, particularly in *La Berceuse*, 'in green with orange hair standing out against a background of green with pink flowers', holding a string which is attached to the cradle beyond the frame of the picture. This portrait, calm and maternal, he thought of as being hung in any fishing boat's cabin as an emblem of home and safe childhood to sailors. There was deep moral purpose in his painting, fully self-realised. His strong colours were used 'to give hope to poor creatures... it is actually one's duty to paint the rich and magnificent aspects of nature. We are in need of gaiety and happiness, of hope and love... I want to say something comforting, as music is comforting.'

In June he had met a lieutenant in the Zouave

regiment named Milliet, to whom he gave drawing lessons. They became fast friends, often visiting the brothels of Arles together. Vincent painted his friend's portrait as well as that of a Zouave bugler. Other portraits from this time include one of Eugéne Boch who visited Vincent at the beginning of September. As usual Vincent was fully aware of the value of his work and had such confidence that his friend Milliet was quite surprised. 'Madam Ginoux,' Vincent told another of his sitters, 'one day your portrait will hang in the Louvre.' In fact, it is in New York's Metropolitan Museum of Art: *L'Arlésienne*, as it is called, is one of the most widely cited works of modern portraiture.

It was also during this frantically hectic September that Vincent experimented with painting out of doors at night. He had been struck by the contrasting colours and quality of light from a café terrace on the place du Forum and wished to capture it. Although his subject was well lit, the canvas on which he worked was not, and he could not satisfactorily mix his colours in the dark. He overcame the problem by planting candles all round the wide brim of his straw hat and others around his easel. It became the unanimous opinion in Arles that he was not merely eccentric, but mad. Mad or no, his *Café Terrace at Night* is a masterpiece of colour composition, and a technical triumph. The experiment had been so successful that the following year, in June 1889, Vincent produced another of his greatest masterpieces, *Starry Night*, which he described appropriately vividly to Theo: 'The sky is greenish-blue, the water royal blue, the ground mauve. The town is blue and violet, the grass is yellow and the reflections are russet-gold down to greenish-bronze. On the blue-green expanse of sky the Great Bear sparkles green and pink, its discreet pallor contrasts with the harsh gold of the grass. Two colourful little figures of lovers in the foreground.'

His interest in the colours of the night found expression in another painting of the busy September of 1888. *The Night Café* is a painting of the interior of the Café de l'Alcazar, which remained open all night and served as a refuge for night-prowlers, drunks and those too poor to stay anywhere else. He described its conception in detail:

> To the great joy of the landlord, of the postman whom I had already painted, of the visiting night-prowlers and of myself, for three nights running I sat up to paint and went to bed during the day. I often think that the night is more alive and more richly coloured than the day. Now, as for getting back the money that I have paid to the landlord by means of my painting, I do not dwell on that, for the picture is one of the ugliest I have done. It is the equivalent, though different, of *The Potato Eaters*. I have tried to express the terrible passions of humanity by means of red and green. The room is blood red and dark yellow with a green billiard table in the middle; there are four citron-yellow lamps with a glow of orange and green. Everywhere there is a clash and contrast of the most disparate reds and greens in the figures of little sleeping hooligans, in the empty, dreary room, in violet and blue. The blood-red and yellow-green of the billiard table, for instance, contrast with the soft tender Louis XV green of the counter, on which there is a pink nosegay. The white coat of the landlord, awake in a corner of that furnace, turns citron-yellow, or pale luminous green.

Whatever he felt about it, and however squalid the place may actually have been, it appears quite cheerful as bar-cafés go.

Vincent still cherished his notion of establishing an artists' colony, convinced that the highest achievement to which modern French art could aspire would be more likely attained by a group than by any individual. His good friend Émile Bernard, of whom he automatically thought in that connection, was on military service, but he learned that Paul Gauguin, at present living at Pont-Aven in Brittany, was ill and in financial difficulties. As one of the most exciting painters of the day, also much under the influence of Japan, he seemed to the over-eager van Gogh a natural candidate for 'abbot' of the community. Gauguin needed first persuading and then financing, and it was inevitably to Theo that his brother looked for moral support and the financial wherewithal. His letters to Theo became full of Gauguin, with an almost coy fussiness about arrangements for him to share Vincent's rented house, which he was decorating to look as he envisaged an artists' centre should be.

Gauguin, whose vanity would scarcely have let him agree to the community idea in the capacity of anything less than its 'abbot', recognised idolatry when he saw it, especially when Vincent, who actually knew him more from reports by Bernard and others than from having seen his work, told him in a letter: 'I always think my own artistic conceptions extremely ordinary when compared to yours.' He saw his chance to be free of his immediate money troubles, but he was suspicious of Theo van Gogh's motives in offering to provide for him, imagining some scheme to exploit him. His hesitancy about accepting served to increase Vincent's eagerness, to the further detriment of his nervous system. By the time Gauguin at length consented, finally persuaded by Theo's agreeing to pay off his current debts and make him a monthly allowance, Vincent was fluttering like a bride-to-be, apprehensive about what Gauguin would think of him and how he would judge his performance. His condition was made worse by renewed over-work, as he strove to complete as many pictures as possible, for 'I am ashamed of it, but I am vain enough to want to make a certain impression on Gauguin with my work.'

'I must beware of my nerves,' he warned, little imagining how they were about to be taxed following the anxiously awaited coming of Paul Gauguin to Arles on 23 October 1888.

Madness and Genius

1888 – 1890

VAN GOGH AND GAUGUIN had met only briefly and occasionally before this, and Vincent had proposed a preparatory exchange of self-portraits. Gauguin's proved to be boldly coloured, reflecting his often arrogant self-confidence. His gaze is returned to the viewer only casually through the corner of his eyes, while his head appears to be turning away. Set on the wall behind Gauguin and to the right is a simple representation of the more modest Émile Bernard, painted largely in line and without modelling, in full profile looking to the left towards the man for whom he had so much admiration - Gauguin. At the bottom left is the inscription, *'les misérables'* -an allusion both to Victor Hugo and to the shared stuggles of artists.

Gauguin, however, shared none of Vincent's ambition to establish a co-operative; his taking advantage of the invitation to establish himself at Arles was wholly selfish. He did not even like the place, describing it as 'the filthiest place in the Midi', and showed no interest in the house which Vincent had worked so hard to prepare against his coming. What he did see was Vincent's untidy way of living and working, the inefficiency of his 'house-keeping' and neglect of his finances. To the former stockbroker and sailor these were abhorrent, and he lost no time in taking charge, dividing their monthly stipends from Theo into weekly allowances, apportioned between food, drink, materials, and 'hygienic excursions' to the local brothels. Then they settled down to paint, Vincent working quickly and intuitively, largely from the subject, Gauguin proceeding slowly and after meticulous preparations from sketches and notes, worked up from his memory. In the evenings they discussed theory, about which they found little to agree. Their respect for one another as executants was high, but with Gauguin insisting on the superior importance of line, as opposed to Vincent's passionate new belief that it was colour which mattered most, their arguments were waged hotly, leaving them both mentally drained.

By 23 December Vincent was admitting that Gauguin was obviously 'a little out of sorts with the good town of Arles, the little yellow house where we work, and especially with me', and wondering whether his friend might not soon decide to leave. He was unaware that Gauguin had already written to Theo asking for the proceeds from the sale of one of his paintings to be sent to him so that he could return to Paris.

In the meantime the two men worked on together as best they could - Vincent producing pictures of extraordinary innovation, while Gauguin did work of little consequence though great confidence. Vincent made the famous paintings of his own chair, yellow, bold and simple, with his tobacco and pipe placed on it, and Gauguin's chair, more fanciful with armrests and painted in red and green, with two books and a burning candle on it. Gauguin did a portrait of Vincent painting one of his favourite subjects, sunflowers. 'It is certainly me,' Vincent said, 'but me gone mad.'

Gauguin seems to have changed his mind about leaving Arles quite so soon, although his relations with Vincent were not much improved. 'Our arguments are terribly *electric*,' wrote Vincent, 'sometimes we come out of them with our heads as exhausted as a used electric battery.' He told Theo of 'grave difficulties to overcome here, for him as well as me. But these difficulties are more within ourselves than outside.' Less than a day after he had written that, disaster struck. During their evening's drinking in the café round the corner Vincent had thrown his glass at Gauguin's head. Gauguin literally carried him home to bed and next day Vincent apologised.

In his book *Avant et Aprés* Gauguin recalled that when he told Vincent that he would leave Arles, Vincent tore out part of a newspaper and handed it to Gauguin. It read, 'The murderer has fled.' On Christmas Eve, the evening after the glass-throwing incident, Gauguin felt he needed a solitary walk, so hurriedly ate his meal and went out.

> I had crossed almost the whole of the place Victor Hugo, when I heard behind me a light step. It was rapid and abrupt, and I knew it well. I turned around just as Vincent was coming at me with an open razor in his hand. I must have looked at him then with a very commanding eye, for he stopped, lowered his head, and turned and ran back towards the house.

Many vivid versions exist of what followed, though no one has been able to substantiate the full story. Most commentators are agreed that Vincent returned home, where he took his razor and cut off the lobe of his left ear - not the entire ear as is generally believed. He then walked to a nearby brothel where he handed the bizarre gift to a prostitute called Rachel, saying 'Keep this object carefully.'

When the police visited The Yellow House they found Vincent unconscious in bed with his ear mutilated, and took him to hospital. Gauguin, who had chosen to spend the night in an hotel for fear of attack, had to convince them that their argument had not caused him to attack Vincent. He telegraphed to Theo who hastened to Arles, returning to Paris a few days later convinced that his brother's days were numbered.

For months Vincent had been working at the height of his powers and had been trying desperately to impress Gauguin with the value of his work. These two factors must certainly figure large in any explanation of Vincent's action. Overwork of such intensity must surely have pushed him beyond the limits of exhaustion. His state, Theo told his fiancée Johanna Bonger, 'was painfully sad to witness, for at times all his sufferings overwhelmed him and he tried to weep but he could not; poor fighter and poor, poor sufferer. For the moment nobody can do anything to relieve his sorrow.' An explanation sometimes advanced for Vincent's behaviour is that he had heard voices in his head urging 'Kill him! Kill him!' during his last argument with Gauguin.

Vincent was restricted to a cell for madmen in the hospital in Arles. The window in it was so high that he was denied the view of the landscape, which might possibly have aided his recovery. Nonetheless, he recovered quickly and left the hospital on 7 January, feeling refreshed. He did not relax from his work, however, and soon began a portrait of Dr Felix Rey, the house surgeon who was still treating his ear. But on 9 February he had a relapse and returned to the hospital. Fear of madness was starting to plague him, exacerbated by the jeers of children in the streets of Arles. When he shouted abuse back at them he was carried off by police back to the hospital and locked into a cell for dangerous inmates. This was followed by a petition from some of the townspeople demanding that he be kept confined. A Protestant minister, Pastor Salles, who had visited Vincent during his previous confinement, told Theo that his brother was sure that if the police had prevented the people of Arles from deliberately tormenting him by crowding around his house and climbing the windows he would have been better able to recover. 'But as for considering myself altogether sane,' Vincent had written to Theo, 'we must not do it. People here who are ill like me have told me the truth. You may be old or young, but there will always be moments when you lose your head. So I do not ask you to say of me that there is nothing wrong with me, or that there never will be.'

At the end of March, Vincent's old painter friend Paul Signac broke a journey and paid him a visit at the hospital. He was able to accompany Vincent for a walk and they managed to enter The Yellow House, despite its being locked, and Signac was able to look at the pictures there and listen to him ramble on about art in the usual way. But Vincent tried to drink the turpentine he kept there for his work, and Signac was left agreeing with Theo that he needed some sort of supervision to prevent his going completely off his head. Vincent confessed that he no longer had the strength or ability to order his life for himself.

Pastor Salles suggested that Vincent enter the asylum at the nearby town of Saint-Rémy-de-Provence. Despite a wild notion that he would be better off in the Foreign Legion, Vincent applied for admission, and with the aid of Pastor Salles and Theo it was arranged. He became an inmate on 8 May, the director, Dr Théophile Peyron, noting in his records that he was subject to acute mania with hallucinations of sight and hearing, and liable to epileptic fits at very infrequent intervals.

During the fifteen months that Vincent had stayed in Arles, between February 1888 and May 1889, he had made over two hundred paintings, a great many of which are now on permanent exhibition in the leading galleries of the world. Understanding that Vincent's only remaining hopes rested in his painting, Theo had requested Dr Peyron to allow his brother to paint out of doors. Peyron, a former naval doctor, knew little of the treatment of mental illness, beyond the desirability of long warm baths twice a week, though his diagnosis of epilepsy is widely thought to have been quite accurate. The therapy Vincent needed most was his painting, and before long he was working regularly once again. He described his fellow inmates as 'beasts in a menagerie', but 'in spite of that people get to know each other very well and help each other when their attacks come on. When I am working in the garden they all come to look, and I assure you they have the discretion and manners to leave me alone - more than the good people of the town of Arles, for instance.' He likened the place to a third-class railway waiting room, with 'some distinguished lunatics who always wear a hat, spectacles and a cane and travelling cloak, almost like a watering place.'

Observing others suffering from varying states of disorder of the mind seems to have helped him to overcome some of his fears about his own condition by removing the feeling of lonely suffering. As he drew and painted in the garden of the asylum his condition began to improve. Before long he was permitted to make excursions into the countryside acompanied by a guard, and in mid-June painted one of his most striking masterpieces, again titled *Starry Night*. It is a whirling cosmic paroxysm, expressive of sublime mysticism, the inexplicable powers of nature possessing a dream-like quality, despite the thoroughly observed realism which dictates the technique. Many have written lengthy interpretations of the picture and have tried to explain its origins, but with a lack of success that is apparently inevitable in relation to a work of such supreme stature. One hint from Vincent, may be worth recording: 'Just as we take the train to Tarascon or Rouen, we take death to reach a star.'

On 6 July Vincent was allowed to go to Arles with a guard in order to collect some canvases to send to Theo. Two days later he suffered another attack which continued to plague him until mid-August. Once again he recovered to produce two intense self-portraits, a study of swirling cypress trees and a portrait of the chief warder, Trabu. For at least two months he remained indoors of his own volition, often painting copies of engravings of works by Rembrandt, Millet, Delacroix, Daumier and Doré, which had been supplied by Theo. He sensed he would suffer a new attack around Christmas, always the worst time of year for his spirits. It came on 24 December, the anniversary of crises with his father, his brother and Gauguin. It lasted until the New Year, soon followed by two more, from 23 January to the 30th and from mid-February to mid-April.

Theo and Johanna Bonger had married in the spring of 1889: it has been suggested by more than one biographer that Vincent's acute disturbance at that time was triggered by the fear that his brother would no longer have the means or inclination to support him. On 1 February 1890 their first child was born. It was a boy, as they had hoped, and they named him Vincent Willem. Vincent was delighted and painted the tender Japonesque *Flowering Almond Tree* as a present for his nephew. No sooner had he completed it than another attack overwhelmed him: 'You will see that it was perhaps what I have done most patiently and best, painted calmly and with a greater sureness of touch. And the next day, down and out like a beast.'

In late January Theo had sent him an article from the *Mercure de France* by the critic Albert Aurier. Entitled *Les Isolés*, it was the first attempt to assess the enormous symbolistic contribution of the work of van Gogh. Vincent was less flattered than overwhelmed at such attention which, he felt, was more than his work alone justified, and seems to have considered Aurier's article a work of art in itself. He told Theo, 'I needn't tell you that I hope to go on thinking that I do not paint like that, but I do see in it how I ought to paint. For the article is very right as far as indicating the gap to be filled, and I think that the writer really wrote it more to guide, not only me, but the other Impressionists as well.' He wrote a well considered response to Aurier, sending a copy to Gauguin, who felt that he should have been the object of Aurier's attentions rather than Vincent.

On 14 February, Theo wrote to Vincent with more good news. One of his paintings, *The Red Vineyard*, had been sold at an avant-garde exhibition in Brussels organised by a group of twenty artists and writers known as *XX*, or *Les Vingt*. The purchaser was the Belgian painter Anna Boch, the sister of Eugéne who had visited Vincent at Arles: she paid 400 francs for it. Though this was not the first nor only sale that van Gogh ever made, as is usually claimed, it was clearly a significant breakthrough. Vincent, however, was not heartened by it and 'feared at once that I should be punished for it; that is how things nearly always go in a painter's life: success is about the worst thing that can happen.'

More and more he was thinking again of the north, of the house at Zundert, of his mother, of his father and of the influences which had impelled him to paint *The Potato Eaters*. For some time he had felt convinced that he was ready to leave Saint-Rémy, but recurring attacks had prevented his doing so. His awareness of his state and of the inexorable running out of his time are movingly conveyed in his painting, done without model, of a blue-clad old peasant seated on a hard chair, his face buried in his clenched hands: its title is *On the Threshold of Eternity*. He thought of joining Gauguin in Brittany, and of returning to Antwerp. Finally his hopes came to rest on his old friend Pissarro, who, unable to offer Vincent a home himself, suggested a solution. He knew of a Dr Paul Gachet who lived in Auvers-sur-Oise, twenty miles from Paris. He was an artistic, sympathetic man, was friends with a number of important artists, and would find Vincent lodgings close enough to his own home for him to give medical help. Vincent's impatience to leave Saint-Rémy grew. Delaying only long enough to execute two highly contrasted flower studies -*The White Roses* and *Vase with Irises* - he left in the middle of May for Paris.

Northwards and Home

1890

BEFORE LEAVING SAINT-RÉMY Vincent had written to Theo insisting that he should make the long journey to Paris alone and on the day before his departure telegraphed Theo to inform him of his time of arrival. Theo, worried about his brother's fitness to travel alone, hardly slept at all that night before their reunion at the Gare de Lyon at ten o'clock on the morning of 17 May. Vincent met two members of his family for the first time. Theo's wife, Johanna van Gogh-Bonger, recalled how she had expected to be confronted by a sick man but found that he looked healthier than Theo, who was suffering from a kidney complaint. After meeting Johanna, Vincent was introduced to his nephew and namesake by Theo. Neither of them spoke a word but simply looked at young Vincent Willem with tears in their eyes. Vincent then turned to his sister-in-law and, pointing towards the cover on the cradle, said tenderly, 'Don't cover him too much in lace, little sister.'

Vincent then spent three extremely busy days in Paris, visiting the Salon and receiving calls from old friends, including Pissarro, Lautrec and good old Père Tanguy. Johanna later set down her memory of that brief period:

> He stayed with us three days, and was cheerful and lively all the time. Saint-Rémy was not mentioned. He went out by himself to buy

olives, which he used to eat every day and which he insisted on our eating too. The first morning he was up very early and was standing in his shirt sleeves, looking at his pictures which covered our walls - in the dining room *The Potato Eaters*, in the sitting room the great *Landscape of Arles* and the *Night View on the Rhone*. Besides, to the great despair of our housekeeper, there were under the bed, under the sofa, in the cupboards in the little spare room, huge piles of unframed canvases.

He and Theo dragged them out and spread them all over the floors to inspect together. It must have been an affecting experience to Vincent to gaze retrospectively on such a range of his moods and emotions, his eager enthusiasms and his numbing despairs. It and the long talks with fellow artists left him too disturbed to do any of the painting he had hoped to manage in the city, whose own bustle added to his agitation and made him glad to leave after the three days, looking forward to the quietness of village life.

Auvers, occupying sloping ground above the placid River Oise and surrounded by oceans of cornfields, attracted him at once, as it has many other artists of his time and since: 'Very beautiful... it is the real country, characteristic and picturesque.' Instead of staying at the inn which Dr Gachet recommended he took a cheaper room at a small eating house run by the Ravoux family (today the Café à van Gogh) five minutes from Dr Gachet's house. Shortly after his arrival he wrote to his brother and sister-in-law, whom he now addressed together: 'I have seen Dr Gachet, who gives me the impression of being rather eccentric, but his experience as a doctor must keep him balanced enough to combat the nervous trouble from which he certainly seems to me to be suffering at least as seriously as I.' Gachet was a widower in his early sixties, who specialised in the treatment of nervous diseases and had written a paper on melancholia, from which he himself no doubt suffered, to judge from Vincent's *Portrait of Dr Gachet*, painted soon afterwards. Vincent added, 'I am ready to believe that I shall end up being friends with him'; and so he did.

Before leaving Saint-Rémy, Vincent had told Theo 'I have more ideas in my head than I could ever carry out without it clouding my mind. The brush strokes come like clockwork.' As usual, he lost no time in getting down to work. He explored the countryside and found great inspiration in it. He also learned that the artist Louis Dumoulin, 'the man who did Japan', was staying at Auvers, and immediately sought him out to speak of Dumoulin's travels in Japan, to where he was soon to return. Vincent's output at Auvers was more prodigious than ever. As well as producing some of his most remarkable landscapes, he painted some of his most startlingly innovative portraits, including that of Gachet, a charming study of the doctor's nineteen-year-old daughter Marguerite at the piano, and one of a peasant girl in a cornfield. Using a palette no less vivid in its richness than he had used for some time, he seemed to find new harmonies that expressed a calmness of mind and a generally improved state of health.

After his hectic passage through Paris, Vincent felt that he would like to see more of Theo, Johanna and young Vincent in the calm atmosphere of Auvers. He had no sooner expressed his wish than on Sunday 8 June they came to visit him. He met them all at the station and presented his namesake with a bird's nest as a gift. On arrival at Dr Gachet's house Vincent occupied himself with his little nephew, showing him the entire house and the large and extraordinary assortment of animals inhabiting the back yard, ranging from cats, dogs and rabbits to ducks and a peacock. It was a glorious day and one which Vincent told his brother he looked forward to repeating.

He continued to work with unbounded enthusiasm throughout June, producing one of his greatest and most striking masterpieces, *The Church at Auvers*, and came to feel optimistic that his attacks would not return. He contemplated holding an exhibition in Paris, and even had notions of accompanying Gauguin to Madagascar, in the unlikely event of Gauguin's suggesting it. Towards the end of the month, however, Theo wrote cautiously to him, afraid to upset him but informing him that young Vincent had become ill, that Johanna was exhausted with sleepless nights and that he himself had once again been quarrelling with his employers and was once more considering setting up as an independent dealer. It did upset Vincent, and despite reassurances from Theo he could not shake off his concern. On Sunday 6 July, at his brother's invitation, he went to Paris, to find to his relief that things had improved and that there was no longer any cause for worry. All the same, Theo and Johanna were still perturbed about the future and there was much agitated conversation, added to the coming and going of visitors, among them Lautrec for luncheon. It left Vincent tired and he took his leave to catch the train back to Auvers without waiting to see his old friend, the Impressionist Armand Guillaumin, who had promised to come.

It was one of Guillaumin's paintings that was soon to precipitate a falling-out with Dr Gachet which hastened the awaiting crisis. On his return to Auvers a new depression seems to have come over Vincent. He wrote to Theo: 'I think we must not count on Dr Gachet *at all*. First of all he is sicker than I am, I think, or shall we say as much, so that's that. Now when one blind man leads another blind man, don't they both fall in the ditch?'

Gachet had a painting of a nude by Guillaumin that Vincent had very much admired and suggested that Gachet have it framed. On finding soon after that he had done nothing about it Vincent flew into a rage. Seeing him put his hand into his pocket as if to take something out, Gachet stared fixedly at him, which Gauguin had done when Vincent had seemed about to attack him in the street in Arles. Vincent removed his empty hand from his pocket, lowered his head and walked away. The following day he visited Gachet as if nothing at all had occurred, and made no reference to the incident.

Vincent's final letters to Theo became full of faltering doom:

It is no slight thing when all of us feel our daily

bread is in danger; it is not a trifle when for other reasons also we feel that our existence is fragile. Back here, I still felt very sad and continued to feel the weight of the storm which threatens you. What can be done? You see, I generally try to be fairly cheerful, but my life too is menaced at its very root, and my steps also are wavering. I feared - not so much, but a little just the same - that being a burden to you, you felt me rather a thing to be dreaded.

He wrote of his recent work. 'These are vast fields of wheat under troubled skies, and I did not need to go out of my way to try to express sadness and extreme loneliness.'

It is usually asserted that Vincent's menacing painting *Crows over the Wheatfields*, with its symbols of life rushing towards a dead end, was his last. This is not the case, though it is certainly one of the very last he did. There is another, which does not fit as conveniently into the romanticised version of Vincent's life and death. It is *Fields under a Stormy Sky*, in which the new colour harmonies that Vincent had begun to explore are more evident and yet do not detract in the slightest from the threatening expressiveness of the sky. Today these two pictures hang side by side in the Rijksmuseum Vincent van Gogh in Amsterdam.

On 25 July Theo wrote to Johanna, whom he had left holidaying in Holland while he returned briefly to Paris on business: 'I have a letter from Vincent which seems quite incomprehensible; when will there come a happy time for him? He is so thoroughly good.'

Two days later Dr Gachet and his daughter watched Vincent leave their home in the late afternoon; they felt that something was wrong. A few hours later he had not returned to eat his supper at the café of the Ravoux family, which was unlike him. A short while after they had had the meal without him the Ravoux saw him staggering back as if he had been drinking, though they had not known him to do so throughout his stay in Auvers. He staggered past, holding his stomach and without so much as acknowledging them. Madame Ravoux asked him what had happened. Leaning momentarily against the billiard table he answered, 'Oh nothing, I am wounded,' and went on to climb the stairs to his attic room.

Gustave Ravoux followed him up, and found him lying on his narrow bed with his face turned to the wall. 'What is the matter with you?' the land-lord asked. 'Look...' replied Vincent, and turned to show a wound at the bottom of his chest. 'But what have you done?' asked Monsieur Ravoux. 'I have shot myself,' was the reply. 'I only hope I haven't botched it.'

The Ravoux immediately sent for the doctor who attended the village twice a week. Vincent had not seen him before, and asked him to send for Dr Gachet. The two doctors applied a dressing but agreed that it would be impossible to extract the bullet, which was lodged near the spine. Vincent was calm and asked Gachet if he could smoke. His friend filled a pipe for him and lit it before placing it in Vincent's mouth, telling him that he would probably be all right. 'Then I will have to do it all over again,' was Vincent's immediate reply.

He had refused to give Gachet his brother's home address in Paris, so Theo did not receive Gachet's note until he went in to work the next morning. In the meantime the Auvers police had come to complain to Vincent that he had commit-ted a breach of the peace. 'What I have done is nobody else's business,' he told them. 'I am free to do what I like with my own body.'

Theo got there as soon as he could. Vincent's first words were sardonic: 'Missed again!' The two brothers spoke together for most of the day. 'Don't cry,' Vincent said, 'I did it for the good of every-body.' Theo managed to send a note to his wife in which he held out hope, telling her that Vincent had enquired about her and the baby; but he knew that there was not long to go. 'Poor fellow,' he wrote, 'fate has not given him much and he has no illusions left. Things are sometimes too hard, he feels so alone.'

Vincent had battled with fate all his life and had

determinedly fought to lead the life of his choice. With equal determination he had decided the time had come to end his life, and had no will to reverse that action even if it had been possible. Theo continued to assure him of a chance of recovery. 'It's no use,' Vincent replied, 'Misery lasts all one's life...' Nearly thirty-six hours after he had shot himself, at one o'clock in the morning, Vincent addressed his last words to Theo. 'I wish I could go home now,' he said in Dutch, and died. He was 37 years old.

In Vincent's pocket Theo found the last letter his brother had begun to write to him: 'Well, my own work, I am risking my life for it and my reason has half-foundered because of it, that's all right... but what's the use?' Also in the pocket was the pistol with which he had shot himself. M. Ravoux recalled that Vincent had asked to borrow it from him to shoot crows.

Vincent was laid in a coffin set on the billiard table downstairs. His friends came to pay their last respects before the coffin was sealed. The local priest refused to allow the Auvers hearse to be used to carry the body of one who had committed suicide, so a replacement had to be borrowed from a neighbouring village.

Three years later Émile Bernard painted a verbal picture of the funeral on that blisteringly hot high summer day when he had walked in procession together with Theo, Lucien Pissarro, Lauzet, Charles Laval, Ravoux, Père Tanguy, Dr Gachet, and a small mingling of other artists and townspeople.

> On the walls of the room where his body lay all his last canvases were nailed, forming something like a halo around him and rendering - by the brilliance or genius which shone from them - his death even more deplorable to us artists. On the coffin a simple white drapery and masses of flowers, the sunflowers he loved so much, yellow dahlias, yellow flowers everywhere. It was his favourite colour, if you remember, the symbol of the light of which he dreamed in the hearts of men as well as in works of art. Near him also his easel, his folding stool and his

brushes had been placed on the floor in front of
the coffin...

At three o'clock the body was removed. His
friends carried it to the hearse. Some of the
assembled people wept. Theodore van Gogh,
who adored his brother and who had always
sustained him in his struggle for art and inde-
pendence, sobbed pitifully without cease...

We arrived at the cemetery, a little new cemetery
dotted with fresh tombstones. It is on a height
overlooking the fields ready for reaping, under a
wide blue sky he might still have loved - maybe -
and then he was lowered into the grave. Who
would not have cried at that moment - the day
was too much to his liking to allow us to cease
thinking that he might still have lived happily.

The grief-stricken Theo, too broken even to
answer the letters of condolence, at length pulled
himself together sufficiently to begin trying to win
his beloved brother a posthumous recognition, in
compensation for that which had never reached
him in life. He approached Albert Aurier, whose
published assessment of Vincent's work had come
when it was already too late to help him, with the
proposal that he write a biography. Theo would
provide all the details and afford access to the 'very
steady correspondence' which the brothers had
kept up for so long.

Aurier agreed eagerly; but that contemporary
work which could have constituted so invaluable a
record, through its blending of Theo's factual
recollections, Vincent's own words, and the young
critic's perceptive analysis, was never to material-
ise. Aurier's existing commitments prevented his
starting on it, and inside two years he had been
carried off by typhoid, at the age of twenty-seven.

In any case, Theo had already pre-deceased
him. His weak constitution, undermined by the
anguish which he could not shake off, was sapped
further by his efforts to get together some sort of
memorial exhibition. The obvious place would

have been Goupil's gallery, but his relationship with his employers had deteriorated severely. They resented his insistence on promoting the works of the Impressionists and Post-Impressionists - Gauguin in particular - for which there was no commercial demand. If he had had enough money, Theo would have established a gallery of his own, which, given better health, might have made him one of art's great entrepreneurs. With his employers' authority to buy works for stock - though without their knowledge - he had made purchases from Gauguin, Sisley, Pissarro, Degas, Redon, Toulouse-Lautrec and others because his fine taste told him that they were important and should be encouraged (though his integrity prevented him from subsidising his own brother at others' expense.)

The time for the Post-Impressionists was not quite ripe, however: Gauguin, too, would have to die (in 1903) before indifference to his work would be swept away. Theo approached one of the greatest of his fellow dealers, Paul Durand-Ruel, who in 1886 had mounted an exhibition of three hundred oils and pastels by 'the Impressionists of Paris', and had persevered without success with the works of such as Renoir and Monet. The buying public's rejection of them had almost bankrupted him, and he was not prepared to put himself at risk again with the even less recognised van Gogh.

The only course Theo saw left to him was to arrange the exhibition in his own apartment. Watched with growing concern by Johanna, he struggled with the immense task of trying to assemble a balanced and representative selection from the hundreds of canvases in his and Père Tanguy's keeping. (From Vincent's ten years' career, more than 800 authentic paintings and some 900 drawings survive today, their numbers swollen by countless fakes.)

The stress and worry of this work exacerbated Theo's ill health and depression, to the point where his employers admonished him once too often. There was a violent argument, and Theo stormed out.

The culminating gesture of resigning was too much for the delicate balance of his mind; the latent insanity in him turned acute in an instant. He struggled restlessly to organise the showing, scribbled plans for founding the artists' community which Vincent had so desired, and groundlessly wired Gauguin in Brittany to say that he was sending the money he needed to go to the tropics. It had all become illusory, and for a time Theo was violent and had to be confined.

When he was recovered enough to travel, Johanna took him to Holland, hoping that his native surroundings would prove therapeutic. The nervous excitement abated, only to be replaced by impenetrable depression. He died less than six months after Vincent, on 25 January 1891, aged thirty-three, from 'overstrain and sorrow'.

He was buried in Holland. Twenty-three years later Johanna had his remains transferred to Auvers, where they were laid next to Vincent's, reuniting for ever the brothers who had meant so much to each other in life.

Vincent van Gogh's fame owes much to Theo. But for his devoted moral and financial support, the legacy of great works would have been far smaller and less developed. So, too, would be the remarkable literary oeuvre which the letters of Vincent van Gogh constitute.

He was very widely read, in several languages, particularly of the novelists of his own century who dealt in themes of social realism and compassion: Charles Dickens, George Eliot, Dostoevsky, Émile Zola.

> I have a more or less irresistible passion for books, and I continually want to instruct myself, to study, if you like, just as much as I want to eat my bread.

He constantly cited literary parallels with art, and believed that the 'thorough study of pictures and the love of books is as sacred as the love of Rembrandt...'

> There is something of Rembrandt in Shakespeare, and of Corregio in Michelet, and of Delacroix in Victor Hugo; and then there is something of

Rembrandt in the Gospel, or something of the
Gospel in Rembrandt...

He wrote those words before embracing art as his
'career', if so obsessed a life can be so termed. It
was not merely a personal credo. Through his great
sequence of letters - nearly 800 of them, covering
eighteen years of his short life - van Gogh set down
what is surely one of the most intense and self-
analytical autobiographies ever written. He speaks
for all artists and their art in his time and since.
What he wrote, what he painted and drew, and
what he was, constitute an inseparable unity of
expression and striving; and it owes much to the
concerned, endlessly receptive Theo's patience
and love.

Do you know what I often think of, about what I
used to tell you in the old days... that even if I did
not succeed, I still believed that what I had been
working towards would be continued. Not directly,
but one is not alone in believing in things that are
true. And what does one matter personally, then!'

Ivy has grown to form a shared coverlet over the
adjacent graves. At almost any time of the year it is
itself overstrewn with yellow flowers which the
many visitors bring as their most fitting tribute to
both of them.

Van Gogh

1853 – 1890

Pastor Theodorus van
Gogh (1822-1885).

Anna Cornelia
Carbentus (1819-1907).

Vincent's parents. They were married in
May 1851 and the painter was the second
of seven children.

The house in Groot Zundert where
Vincent was born in the room at the top
right of the picture. The house was
demolished in 1903.

The church and graveyard at Zundert. Built in 1806. Theodorus was pastor and his first stillborn child, Vincent Willem, was buried here. Later Vincent and Theo were baptised here.

Grave of Vincent Willem who died at birth in 1852.

A very early drawing (1780) of Groot Zundert. The presbytery is the second house.

Vincent van Gogh's entry in the Register of Births 1853, No.29, 30 March; the same number and day as his stillborn brother of the same name one year earlier.

Early drawings dated January 1862 when Vincent was not yet nine years old. Comparison with the bridge below, a drawing also dated January 1862, and the dog opposite, dated December 1862, has caused controversy over their authenticity.

The Bridge (1862). Bridges obviously interested the painter and formed the subject for many of his later works.

Vincent van Gogh c. 1866, aged about thirteen. The earliest known photograph.

Farm and Waggon Shed (1864). This drawing was a gift to his father on his birthday on 8 February.

The Dog (1862).

Anna Cornelia (1855-1930).

Vincent van Gogh's sisters and brothers.

Elizabeth Huberta (1859-1936).

Wilhelmien Jacoba (1862-1941).

Cornelis Vincent (1867-1900).

Theodorus (Theo) (1857-1891).

Interior of Goupil's Gallery, The Hague, where Vincent worked from 1869.

Uncle Cent (abbreviated from Vincent) who got him the position at Goupil's and was a great influence on the young Vincent.

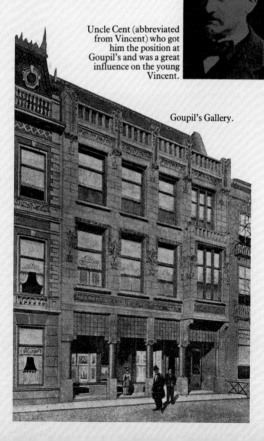

Goupil's Gallery.

Vincent aged about eighteen at the time
of working for Goupil & Co.

This drawing of the canal dates from Vincent's
time in The Hague working for Goupil.

This sketch of Ramsgate was done shortly
after Vincent had arrived on 17 April 1876 to
take up a teaching post on trial and unpaid.

High Street, Welwyn.
Ivy Cottage
was a small boarding
school where his sister
Anna taught French.
Vincent walked here
from London.

The house of Mr Jones in Isleworth where Vincent
was engaged as 'a kind of curate' in July 1876.

A view at Isleworth in the 19th century.

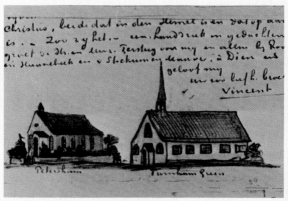

The churches of Petersham and Turnham Green
sketched on a letter at the end of 1876.

A drawing of the presbytery and church at Etten
where the family now lived and his father was
pastor.

A pit in the Borinage, the bleak mining district near Mons in southern Belgium.

Miner with a Shovel (1879).

Vincent arrived in the Borinage in December 1878 and worked as an evangelist, giving bible classes and visiting the poor and sick. His time here was one of dire poverty, suffering miserable deprivation in the most appalling conditions.

The Miners' Return (1879).

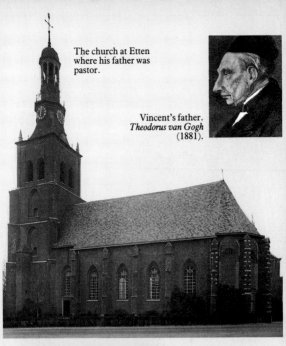

The church at Etten where his father was pastor.

Vincent's father. *Theodorus van Gogh* (1881).

Kee Vos, Vincent's cousin, and her son. The artist fell in love with her in 1881 and suffered his second humiliating rejection in love.

Anton Mauve (1838-1888). Vincent visited the painter, a distant relative married to a cousin, and received advice and help from him. Inevitably they quarrelled and parted.

Mother and Child (1883). After his rejection by Kee Vos,
Vincent found solace with Clasine Maria Hoornik
(1850-1904). Sien, as Vincent called her, was a prostitute.
They met in 1882 and remained together for eighteen months or so.

A contemporary print of the district hospital in The Hague
where Vincent was admitted in June 1882 for treatment of
gonorrhea.

Fish-drying at Scheveningen (1882), a water colour he was later to give to Margot Begemann.

A perspective frame, modelled on Dürer's device, shown here in a letter to Theo.

In August 1882, Vincent began to work in oils, and in another letter to Theo he sketched his palette. 'I limited myself to simple colours.'

Girl in White leaning against a Tree (1882). One of Vincent's early oil paintings.

The Presbytery at Nuenen (1883). Vincent's father had been appointed pastor here in 1882 and remained until his death in 1885. Vincent arrived in December 1883 and at first used the laundry room as his studio.

Margot Begemann. Ten years older than Vincent, she attempted suicide for love of him, the only woman who ever really loved him.

Anton Kerssemakers, an enthusiastic amateur painter and friend who took lessons from Vincent at Nuenen.

The Loom (1884) painted at Nuenen. Van Gogh constantly returned to 'work' as a basic theme in his paintings.

Anthon van Rappard, a well-to-do art student whose five-year friendship stimulated him, but ended in a quarrel.

The Potato Eaters (1885). This extraordinary and exceptional painting, completed at Nuenen, is often referred to as van Gogh's earliest 'masterpiece'.

Self-Portrait (1885). This, one of many self-portraits of the artist, was painted during his time in Antwerp.

Antwerp. Arriving late in November 1885, Vincent took a room here at 194 rue des Images (now 224 Longue rue des Images). Second building from the left.

Vincent's entrance card to the Academy of Art in Antwerp.

Backs of Old Houses in Antwerp (1885).
The artist painted this view from his
window in the room at 194 rue des Images.

An example of Vincent's handwriting in this
urgent surprise note on his arrival in Paris in
February 1886 to his brother Theo, requesting
they meet at mid-day at the Louvre.

Mon cher Theo, ne m'en veux pas d'être venu tout d'un trait.
J'y ai tant réfléchi & je crois que de cette manière nous
gagnons du temps. Serai au Louvre à partir de midi ou
réponse s.v.p pour savoir à quelle heure tu pourrais
venir dans la salle carrée. Quant aux frais, je te le
répète cela revient au même. J'ai de l'argent de reste celui
va sans dire et avant de faire aucune dépense je désire
te parler. Nous arrangerons la chose tu verras.
Ainsi : viens y le plutôt possible. je te serre la main
t. à t. Vincent

A general view of Paris from an early photograph.

54 Rue Lepic. Vincent stayed here in Theo's apartment from June 1886 to February 1888.

A sketch of Vincent working at his easel by Émile Bernard.

Van Gogh studied at the studio of Fernand Cormon on the Boulevard de Clichy. The group here shows his friends, Émile Bernard (arrowed) at th back and, on the stool in the foreground, Toulouse-Lautrec.

Boulevard de Clichy (1887)

Émile Bernard (1868-1941). A self-portrait of the artist and friend of Vincent.

Henri de Toulouse-Lautrec (1864-1901). Another close friend from his time in Paris

The 'Yellow House' at Arles where Vincent lived from May 1888.

Paul Gauguin (1848-1903).
Arriving 23 October 1888, he
lived with Vincent in the
'Yellow House'.
The relationship was often
difficult and even violent.

Vincent's *Chair and Pipe* (1888),
famous picture from the Arles
period.

Gauguin's painting of Vincent at work in November 1888. 'It is
certainly me, but me gone mad.'

The Night Café (1888). 'I have tried to express the idea that the café is a place where one can ruin oneself, go mad, or commit a crime.'

Self-Portrait with Bandaged ear (1889). Painting himself in the mirror, reversing the image, has led to the popular misconception that it was his right ear that was severed. In fact it was the lower portion of his left ear that he cut off after a row with Gauguin and gave to a local prostitute.

Starry Night (1889).

The Saint-Paul-de-Mausole asylum in Saint-Rémy where Vincent was admitted for voluntary confinement on 8 May 1889.

An advertisement for Saint-Paul's.

Corridor in the asylum.

The hydrotherapy bath.

Vincent's cell at Saint-Paul's asylum.

Drawing of the gardens at Saint-Rémy.

The vestibule.

This picture of the vestibule
was painted by Vincent,
omitting the bars shown in
the photograph (left).

The fountain at Saint-Paul's asylum.

Dr Gachet's house at Auvers.
Inset - Dr Paul Gachet.

Dr Paul Gachet (1890). Vincent's portrait of his medical adviser and friend in his last days at Auvers.

The Church at Auvers (June 1890).

Fields under a Stormy Sky (July 1890). 'I did not have to go out of my way to express sadness and extreme loneliness.'

Ravoux's restaurant where Vincent lived at the time of his death. Arthur Gustav Ravoux, the proprietor, is seated on the left. Ravoux innocently loaned the pistol with which the painter shot himself in the chest.

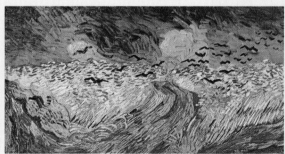

Crows over the Wheatfield (July 1890). This great masterpiece is often suggested as the painter's last canvas. Certainly it was painted just before his death, and in such a place Vincent shot himself late on Sunday afternoon, 27 July 1890.

The room in Ravoux's restaurant where Vincent van Gogh died, 1.30 a.m., Tuesday, 29 July 1890.

Registration of the painter's death.

Theo's formal notification on behalf of the family of his brother's death. His grief never left him. Six months later he lapsed into depression, dying on 25 January 1891 from 'overstrain and sorrow'.

Self-Portrait (May 1890). The last self-portrait and considered by many to be the finest.

The simple gravestones at Auvers-sur-Oise. At almost any time of the year they are strewn with yellow flowers which the many visitors bring as their most fitting tribute.

A charcoal portrait by Dr Gachet of the artist on his deathbed.

ACKNOWLEDGEMENTS

The author and publishers would like to thank the following for their kind
permission in supplying the quotations and illustrations in this book.

Quotations:

New York Graphic Society Books / Little, Brown and Company, Boston
Thames and Hudson Ltd., London

Illustrations:

Collection Mrs. A.R.W. Nieuwenhuizen Segaar, The Hague
BBC Hulton Picture Library, London
Clichés des Musées Nationaux, Paris
Courtauld Institute Galleries, London (Courtauld Collection)
H.P. Bremmer Collection, The Hague
Michael and Mollie Hardwick
Municipal Museum, Breda
Collection, The Museum of Modern Art, New York
Reproduced by courtesy of the trustees, National Gallery, London
National Museum Vincent van Gogh, Amsterdam
Collection, State Museum Kröller-Müller, Otterlo, Netherlands
Mrs. Tersteeg, The Hague
Yale University Art Gallery, Bequest of Stephen Carlton Clark B.A. 1903,
New Haven, Connecticut
Evergreen Lives Archive